GUTS AND GLORY

Praise for the book

'*Guts and Glory* is a rich collection of real-life stories of 20 entrepreneurs. It will become a valuable teaching resource for entrepreneurship educators in India.'

—Harkesh Mittal, Head, National S & T
Entrepreneurship Development Board

'*Guts and Glory* will go a long way in spreading the entrepreneurial spirit among younger generations by igniting their minds.'

—Pramod Chaudhari, Executive Chairman,
Praj Industries Limited

GUTS AND GLORY

20 inspiring stories of graduates from SIBM Pune who made their own future

RUPA

First published by
Rupa Publications India Pvt. Ltd 2014
7/16, Ansari Road, Daryaganj
New Delhi 110002

Sales Centres:
Allahabad Bengaluru Chennai
Hyderabad Jaipur Kathmandu
Kolkata Mumbai

Copyright © SIBM Pune 2014

All rights reserved.
No part of this publication may be reproduced, transmitted,
or stored in a retrieval system, in any form or by any means,
electronic, mechanical, photocopying, recording or otherwise,
without the prior permission of the publisher.

ISBN: 978-81-291-2370-1

First impression 2014

10 9 8 7 6 5 4 3 2 1

This book is sold subject to the condition that it shall not, by way of trade
or otherwise, be lent, resold, hired out, or otherwise circulated, without the
publisher's prior consent, in any form of binding or cover other than that in
which it is published

CONTENTS

Foreword vii
Introduction ix

1. And Then he Moved his Cheese — 2
2. Born to Win — 16
3. The Maverick Entrepreneur — 24
4. Pitcher Perfect — 44
5. Time to Move On — 54
6. Riding the Airwaves — 66
7. Perseverance Personified — 76
8. Never Give Up On Your Dreams — 84
9. 'Raising a Toast to the Spirited' — 100
10. Voice that Inspires — 108
11. On the Spice Trail — 118
12. Risk is a Perception — 132
13. Helping Hand — 142
14. Able to Enable — 152
15. Circle of Life — 166
16. Words' Weaver — 178
17. King of High — 188
18. Rules of Engagement — 198
19. She Fills in the Blanks — 208
20. Flight of Enterprise — 216

FOREWORD

PAST AND PRESENT CREATE OUR FUTURE

The last few years have been immensely exciting for Symbiosis Institute of Business Management (SIBM) Pune. There is joy at the way things are happening and jubilation at the way we are making them happen. This book is one more example of both joy and jubilation. I get immense pride in seeing more and more of our alumni turning to entrepreneurship instead of jobs and it's a pleasure capturing their thrilling entrepreneurial journeys in this exciting book.

This book has been a revelation of sorts for me. For a good part of its 36-year history, SIBM Pune has prided itself on a 100 per cent placement record, but I have been completely overwhelmed by the number of entrepreneurs we have produced along the way. As Director, I am now convinced more than ever that top B-schools like ours can and should lead the way in shifting the focus from creating job-seekers to creating job-creators.

I am sure that the book will carry a similar message to all the readers—students, teachers, parents, administrators and others. While there is absolutely nothing against taking up jobs, it's just a matter of taking calculated risks at the right point of time in their lives and these wonderful youngsters can start creating jobs for others and wealth for themselves. If there is one thing India desperately needs at this point in time, it is more and more of them. I sincerely believe that this book takes one small but determined step in that direction.

I thank Padma Bhushan awardee Dr S.B. Mujumdar, Founder President, and Dr Vidya Yeravdekar, Principal Director of Symbiosis Society, for their constant encouragement and support to the endeavour. I acknowledge with thanks the contribution of all the entrepreneurs, writers, editors and designers for making this book so exciting. And finally, thanks to the person who conceived the book and saw it through—our Head of Faculty for Entrepreneurship, Professor. Vinod Shastri.

Before I end, I must elaborate on the title of this Foreword. All the gripping entrepreneurial stories of our past students have been captured by the present (recent graduates of SIBM Pune) to create a powerful repository of inspiration for the future generations.

Dr Vivek Sane
Director
SIBM Pune

INTRODUCTION

It would be unfair not to acknowledge the inspiration for this book—*Stay Hungry Stay Foolish*, written by Rashmi Bansal. It has been a favourite since I first read it. The amazing array of alumni entrepreneurs of SIBM Pune offered us a similar opportunity.

Dr Vivek Sane is one of those exceptional bosses who give immense space to his team members. He was super quick in approving the project. Thereafter, we promptly put together a crack team of our entrepreneurship students that was finally led by Varun Tejwani and Dhruvish Thakkar, who took over from Niket Khaitan and Modak Sarda. If you like this book, the credit goes entirely to this amazing team.

It was just a matter of days before Varun and Dhruvish put in place a writing team. The entire process was planned like an independent venture. There was no greater pleasure for us as teachers to watch them apply all the knowledge they had gained from their institute. I feel extremely proud to admit that I soon became incidental to the entire process as the students owned the project, showing true entrepreneurial spirit. The contributions of all these wunderkinds are acknowledged with their names at appropriate places.

Vinod Shastri
Deputy Director
SIBM Pune

JAGDISH KINI
Enterprise 5c

After an enviable career in the corporate world, Jagdish Kini turned into an entrepreneur. Today, he heads several ventures right from his flagship consultancy firm to m-commerce start-ups and more.

༶

AND THEN HE MOVED HIS CHEESE

Aravind Haridas and Divya Sharma

After reaching the pinnacle of his corporate career as Executive Director and CEO of Bharti Airtel, Jagdish Kini decided to move his cheese. Having stepped into the shoes of an entrepreneur, he is taking his illustrious career forward with twice the enthusiasm of someone half his age and even less experience.

Jagdish is an entrepreneur with multiple ventures in hand. He is playing several roles and taking up various responsibilities in the many companies he owns—Enterprise 5C (E5c), his flagship consulting firm, provides management consulting and advisory services. Apart from that, his ventures range from m-commerce start-ups to healthcare innovations. He is also mulling over the idea of upgrading the skill-sets of senior personnel in the industry and at B-schools through simulation programmes in various aspects of management. Bringing the benefits of technology to the masses is his mission, and apart from his own businesses, he also helps mentor other budding entrepreneurs, hand holding their businesses and helping them pass the incubation phase.

Life has been an eventful journey for this gentleman who

was born to a middle class family originally from Tonse village near Udupi in Karnataka. 'My father came to Mumbai in 1942 and started working for Burma Shell. He knew the importance of a good education and always pushed his kids to excel in studies. Though he was doing moderately well compared to his peers in those days, funding the professional education of four children was not an easy task and it was during this time that we learnt to thrive on scarce resources.'

Decades later, he has become a true Mumbaikar. Hear the man: 'I have spent almost 35–36 years of my life here. I never bunked school but, at the same time, I was not the most studious kid in the class. The benchmarks set at home were very high because of my elder sister and my younger brother. Coming among the top five in class was the least that was expected of me and I managed to do that pretty well, every time,' says Jagdish. It is not surprising to hear this from a man of his calibre; however, what was surprising was how he always pursued a fine balance in life, ensuring that he did not miss out on things he was passionate about.

He was a bit of a dreamer as a child. 'I had many childhood dreams, and to be a fighter pilot was one. A vocational counsellor in school told me that I could either become a great surgeon or carpenter. My father also wanted me to become a doctor because he thought I might as well use the books that my sister was using to complete her degree. I tried but I could not make it. I finally took up pure sciences in Parle College, Mumbai.'

'Like most of my contemporaries, I too, dreamed of getting a good job after graduation in an MNC although my entire family is into banking. My father put me through a grill after graduation—he would give me ₹10 every day, ₹5 for the bus journey and ₹5 for food and asked me to hunt for a job. Every day I would go to Nariman Point and find information about vacancies in the offices. One fine day, I applied to Siemens. Luckily, I cleared their entrance test. I was put into their switchboard factory in Kalwa.'

'During those days, I used to appear for MBA entrance exams. I always used to clear the written exam but got blasted in the group discussions. MBA institutes in those days preferred IITians and Stephanians. Through Siemens, I was supposed to go to Germany when I got an admission offer from SIBM Pune. I thought if I decided go to Germany, I would never get a chance to get a post-graduate degree. I decided to take up the seat. It was one of the best decisions that I've made, because in addition to the degree, I found my life partner, my love, and my support at SIBM. I guess that's destiny.'

His corporate career, spanning close to three decades, would be a matter of envy for anyone aspiring to be successful. His corporate career started with Procter & Gamble (P&G) India where he joined as a management trainee in finance. After a long nine-year stint he moved to L'Oreal India from where he was headhunted to become the Managing Director of Gillette India at the very young age of 39.

Jagdish had a great time at P&G and considers it as a great school of learning for him. 'I had a great set of bosses to learn from: Gurcharan Das, Bharat Patel and Sumeet Bhattacharya. Gurcharan believed in people and experimented a lot and he said you must pick up guys who have the potential to become GMs in the future and give them job rotation. Gurcharan taught me about the value system being the checklist of every decision in life. Then there was Meherwan Tambuwala who made me understand how you need to attack the issue and not the person'.

His term in L'Oreal taught him the importance of being flexible. 'You should be flexible in your thinking. If a target which was agreed upon is not achievable anymore because of the circumstances, there is no point in being upset about it.' He also learnt that simple products can be made very effective through technology. 'I believed a shampoo was a shampoo until I was introduced to L'Oreal. If I have to sell hair colour to salons, I had to understand what the salon business is. I actually went through a training course on hair colouring. You need to understand what your product is, know what its touch and feel is.'

What is worth mentioning here is that his later positions, whether it be in L'Oreal or Airtel, were more of greenfield projects than run-of-the-mill corporate jobs. 'A greenfield project, to me, is an entrepreneurial stint with someone else's money. At P&G, I learnt to build brands, at L'Oreal and Gillette, I learnt to build companies and at Airtel, I learnt to build an industry. I feel truly blessed for getting those opportunities.' He was one of the key members of the team which started the subsidiary for L'Oreal in India, and Airtel was in its infancy when he joined it. 'Mobile Telephony in India was then a greenfield industry'.

Understandably, for Jagdish, his stint with Airtel was the golden period in his life, 'I enjoyed every bit of my corporate life. The time I was with Airtel—I call it the golden period because I got to challenge myself every day. In the telecom industry what works today is passé tomorrow, and at the same time success begets success. The more we succeeded, the more challenges we started taking up and I had a fantastic team at

Airtel. I was handling all the circles from Maharashtra through Goa up to Kanyakumari. Every CEO in every circle I was managing was a godsend. We focused on taking the benefits of technology to customers. The executive team challenged each other and managed each other brilliantly. We created nationwide benchmarks for Airtel as well as for the entire telecom industry. Here was an opportunity where we could change the way we live and make a difference to the way the average Indian lives if we get it right. What I liked about Sunil Mittal was his vision. In spite of having just one circle, he had such a large vision that I instantly wanted to be a part of that vision. I took everything as a challenge—the industry, vision, concepts and managerial skills.'

LESSONS FROM FAILURE

Jagdish was in one of the most enviable positions in the corporate world of India when he quit Airtel. The company had reached its greatest heights under his leadership. He did fulfil the dreams he had seen as a young lad during his MBA and had perhaps achieved what every MBA graduate aspires to achieve in a corporate world. Soon after quitting, he realized he needed to wear his tie and go out every morning. This is how E5C was born.

'E5c is an abbreviation for Enterprise 5C. At E5c we spell success with 5 Cs. The 5 Cs are the basic tenets of my company—Character, Commitment, Consistency, Communication and Collaboration. I wanted to set a vision for myself and give back to the industry. It had to be more than consulting. I also do a lot of mentoring for budding entrepreneurs under E5C free of cost because I don't want them to make the mistakes that I made.'

'It was a one-man show in the beginning. It soon began to grow and I took an office space on rent in Bangalore. Most of our projects are strategic and we work with the Chief Experience Officers (CXOs) in companies. We also have projects for organization capability-building and leadership development. We help companies pick fast-track candidates and over a period of a year, we help them become future leaders. I try to leverage my rich experience with the telecom sector and hence, take up a lot of projects in this sector. Through exhaustive customer understanding, we have developed a Customer Satisfaction Enhancement Model for Airtel. We have also built an Employee Empowerment Indices and Satisfaction Index Model for the strategic partners for Airtel. We have a department which helps in recruitment. That's an ongoing thing and we cater to the middle- to higher-level positions. This started initially as a help to our clients and then became a business unit.'

'Initially, the projects were staggered. For example, the Airtel project was my first project and I worked on measurement of customer satisfaction for them. I had a team in Airtel that was working with me. It was very easy for me; all I had to do was actually fly to Delhi and help them conceptualize the whole thing. It was easy in the beginning and I managed with one person for some administrative assistance. Then as E5C grew, I recruited more people. Recruitment was never a problem as I had managed to build enough goodwill in the past that people would actually want to work with me again. We clinched a big project when Tata gave us a mandate to turn around some of their telecom circles. We have done projects for Vodafone,

3M, Ferrero Rocher, Atria Convergent Technologies, and Aircel among others'.

Failure is an inevitable part of every entrepreneurial journey and Jagdish's story is no exception. He co-founded a company called MyDunia Networks. MyDunia Networks, Jagdish describes, 'was about an online platform where you could create your own space. Through the mobile phone you could interact with the internet through an SMS. You could send a document stored in your space on the platform with an alert message to reach your contacts by e-mail/phone. It was similar to a virtual assistant. It had immense possibilities. It was all about managing the web through a handset. We had a test launch in Karnataka. We held a press conference in the afternoon, and by evening it had become quite a success and we had around 500 hits in a matter of few hours. And then, issues erupted and by 8.30 p.m. the site was closed down. Our strategic partner viewed us more as a competitor rather than a partner and the venture failed. The cash burn was not worth the fight.'

The failure helped Jagdish in more than one way. First of all, it served as an eye-opener to him. After years of corporate life, he realized what the job of an entrepreneur was. 'MyDunia Networks definitely could have been handled better. I was not completely involved in that company, which was my mistake. I should have handled the politics and people of our strategic partner better. I have managed enough people in the past 30 years but I have realized managing people of a strategic partner is always a challenge. It's about working as equals, despite the fact that the strategic partner was many times the size of our company. Understanding technology is very important for me. I now ask more questions than I asked before. I hope to develop a better understanding of technology in my future ventures.'

The experience also taught Jagdish to be more cautious and he has now become more careful and discreet while choosing his strategic working partners because even a signed contract could not help him save his MyDuniya venture. He also believes that youngsters holding responsible business positions probably do not show enough respect for the experience and values the experienced people in the industry come with. Through his own experience he has come to terms with the fact that most people respect the chair a person holds more than the person, and are opportunistic in their approach.

The failure didn't deter Jagdish and he soon started talking about his new plans enthusiastically. 'I am a part of another company now, and it is an IT services company in healthcare. We are trying to build an entire environment in healthcare—it is called Health5C. The objective is to promote healthcare while bringing down the costs associated with it. So by helping the citizens remain healthy we would bring down the costs of healthcare by running hospitals and pharmacies more efficiently and simultaneously benefiting insurance companies. We would also take healthcare to the rural parts of India. The motto is "Education to bring in awareness to bring in action to bring in care."

One magazine described him as *Kini—The Builder* and that really sums him up. He quit the industry at his peak because he didn't see his role continuing there. Initially, he missed managing a company after leaving Airtel but his real passion was building. He saw that passion of building coming true in E5c. 'Every time I work with a new client on a new project I build something. Therefore, my vision was not connected to the top-line or bottom-line of my company. It has to be taken care of, but 30 per cent or 60 per cent or 78 per cent, margins are mere numbers. What matters is what have you built—has it made a difference to society, and is it sustainable?

For someone who has been managing really aggressive targets all his corporate life, success carries an altogether different meaning now. 'I also do entrepreneurship counselling and there are many people I don't charge, so if I don't charge there is no revenue. There are youngsters who call me up and take career advice—I haven't charged a single rupee for career counselling, the number must have been 60–70 till now. It's the investment in people, making sure the future of the country is in safe hands. Now I feel that deriving satisfaction out of a task at hand is about managing expectations. So when you have no expectation, everything is satisfactory. So it is all about whether I have enjoyed every single day, every project and every client. If I feel I have contributed to a client's success, it gives me enough satisfaction. I only compete with myself now. I have enjoyed my corporate career phase in life and am enjoying this phase too. Certainly, there is more time available here and probably that's because I don't take up too many projects at one time.'

Jagdish's world consists of his wife, two daughters, mother and mother-in-law. His wife, Anjali, whom he met in SIBM Pune, worked in several multinational companies (MNCs) in the areas of Finance and IT. She found it difficult to balance work with home and hence decided to quit work and opened a recruitment agency called Orion Consultants in Mumbai. She gave it up when Jagdish had to move across countries. Jagdish considers her the driving force behind his success and their current enterprise.

'Our older daughter is a post-graduate from Tata Institute of Social Sciences (TISS) and worked for two years before deciding to change careers. She now teaches dance to young children. Her husband owns a franchisee of Volkswagen. Our younger daughter completed her BBM, Bachelor's in Business Management, degree from Christ College in Bangalore and is right now interning with Accenture. She wants to work for some years and then pursue a management degree.'

SUCCESS MANTRAS

'First and foremost, I have always believed that the customer is the one who decides what we as an organization need to do. If the customer wants it, we better deliver it. So it is "customer customer customer". Second is innovation. We should always question ourselves—"Why are we doing this? Is there a better way of doing this?" Third is the primacy of the individual: Respect for the person. Do not attack the person, attack the issue. It's the process which has a flaw. Identify the flaw and rectify that. So separate the person and the issue.

'My leadership style has always been "honest, open and transparent". In times of taking the blame, take it on your chin first and in times of giving credit, give it to your people first. For me, it is as simple as that—leading from the front, being honest, open and transparent is very important. I would never ask my people to do what I would not do. People who work with you are not stupid. They are as intelligent as you are and some of them are even more.

'I've always believed in talk the talk and walk the talk. What is "talk the talk and walk the talk"? This is a new concept I brought in long back. Talk the talk is for me very important because it is my personal leadership style. When I talk the talk, I repeat my goal vision. I realized that I cannot communicate something convincingly if I don't believe in it. It is my strength. So when I talk the talk, I ask myself if I still believe in my goal or not. If the answer is yes then I do communicate it to others and it is after this that I walk the talk. Thus, talk the talk is to ask myself about my continuing belief in my vision/goals and walk the talk means to achieve that vision/goal.

'I've always recruited people who are better than me. I've recruited a lot of youngsters because the youngsters make you think, they have the courage to ask you "why"—that's where innovation comes in. I've always promoted people who did a great job, and I do not bother to check their degrees while considering them for promotions. For me it is all about performance. In Airtel, I had a bias—in terms of numbers, I had more females than males in the company, strictly because I felt they were more committed, more honest and they delivered consistently.

'I think entrepreneurs should believe in themselves, in what they want to achieve in life. There is a reason for everyone to be alive in this world and you have to understand what that reason is. Understanding this will keep you moving forward in the direction of your goal. You could do that by being an entrepreneur or by being something else.

'Wealth will come sooner or later. Do not make wealth your primary focus, look for other goals. People look at successful entrepreneurs and only see the wealth they have amassed.

They don't see the struggle that they went through before they achieved success.

'I get disturbed when I see people taking shortcuts. There is no shortcut for success. You have to go through the toil and build everything brick by brick. And ultimately, everything comes down to character.

'My company stands for 5 Cs. I spell success with 5 Cs—Character, Commitment, Consistency, Collaboration and Communication. I firmly believe that anybody who can follow the 5 Cs will have a very strong value system and I am willing to underwrite their success. I have made enough mistakes in my 30 years in the industry. It is an integral part—thus by all means make mistakes but don't repeat the mistakes. That's my message to the younger generation. Do not hesitate to make mistakes.

'A business idea has to be practical and achievable. While the idea needs to be innovative, more importantly, there has to be a space where it can operate. The most critical factor, however, is the entrepreneurial passion and the commitment to make it work. Business plans can always be altered and fine-tuned.

'When people come to me with their business plans, a lot of times I act dumb and tell them that I don't understand their plans. And when they try to explain they realize they are getting stuck. That's how I keep pushing entrepreneurs to explore. I don't offer many ideas. Very often, youngsters come to me with brilliant ideas. The ideas are so wild on occasions that I am simply taken aback.

'I ask questions to make other people think because that's when the person owns the idea, and the commitment is stronger. My questioning works in a way that I get the person to explore the side I want him to explore.'

VISHWAS MAHAJAN
Compulink

Vishwas Mahajan's life is a rare story of courage, willpower, talent and the ability to conquer obstacles that come one's way. The former CEO and co-founder of Compulink Systems Ltd is now engaged in helping budding entrepreneurs, a natural step for a person who has seen life in all its shades during his eventful journey.

ల

BORN TO WIN

Team SIBM

Humble beginnings offer very little space for glorious dreams. Reconciling with the desire for a run-of-the-mill existence that includes meeting one's basic necessities is a commonplace ambition. But a young Vishwas Mahajan was different. He knew he had it in him to look beyond the obvious and achieve more than expected. This he did, not by earning good money in a cushy corporate job but by building an empire of his own.

Vishwas was born in Nashik, a small town in Maharashtra. His father was a primary school teacher who passed away two years after his birth. When he was seven, his mother remarried. Detached from his mother, he moved to Pune to his granduncle's place, who offered him a place to stay. Thus began a new journey of his life. His anchor, his granduncle, was an avid Gandhi follower who aspired to unite India through Hindi. Young Vishwas was greatly influenced by his sheer determination but he saw the practical side of it. It didn't pay.

His superior intellect won him a scholarship that fully funded his education at Sanjeewan Vidyalaya, an elite school in Panchgani. Initially, he felt like a misfit among the kids of the rich and the famous. Gradually, however, the awkwardness vanished and he became a part of the crowd. Until the completion of his 12th standard, he was living inside a cocoon. Then, reality struck. Once more.

Vishwas's fine academic record secured him a place in Walchand College of Engineering in Sangli which was part of Shivaji University. But his financial compulsions prevented him from taking admission. So, he exercised the only option he had: which is, join R.K. Talreja College in Ulhasnagar where the fee was less. While completing his education, Vishwas started scouting for ways to earn. He applied for bank clerical exams and cleared the written part. He also tried his luck with management exams. To his delight, he got selected in Jamnalal Bajaj Institute of Management Studies (JBIMS) and SIBM Pune. He wanted to join the latter, but paying the fee was an uphill task. The fee was ₹3600 for two years, which, for Vishwas, was a huge amount. His dreams were shattered, and he was left with no option barring that of making a compromise. During his interview for the bank clerk's job, he stated his compulsion. This is where destiny intervened. The interviewers from the Bank of Maharashtra suggested that he should take a bank loan and follow his dream. That proved to be the turning point.

The Bank of Maharashtra sanctioned him the loan of ₹3600 after his distant relatives became guarantors. That is how journey with SIBM began. Many of his classmates wanted to be consultants during that time but his objective was clear. He wanted to get a job that paid well. He never even thought about a possible future as an entrepreneur during his days at SIBM. After he acquired an MBA degree, he was one of the three students who got placed with PSI Data Systems in Pune in 1984. As it was a start-up, the pay was irregular. But that didn't dampen his spirit. He, in fact, learned a lot from his stint at the

PSI where he worked for one-and-a-half years. It was during that period that he met Uday Kothari through common friends. Kothari was working with Zenith, another Pune-based company. Later, Uday and Vishwas would go on to establish Compulink.

After his tenure with PSI, he worked with Digital Equipment Corp from 1986 to 1988, the then giant in mini-computers. Thereafter, he was offered a job for ₹11 lakhs at Key Information Technology, a systems integration firm in Dubai. The lifestyle and monetary benefits were vastly different in Dubai where he worked for more than five years from 1988 to 1994, but it was here that he felt his true calling was a start-up in India. His three jobs had given him a good idea of what his company should and should not be all about regardless of the business it chose to be in. He was getting married around this time, and he also communicated his plans to his to-be wife. Being a classical dancer, she welcomed this decision also because her vocation had far better scope in India.

If it were up to him, he would have liked to pursue his dream right away. But unfortunately, Uday was dealing with the loss of his father. So, for a year, they left their plan on the backburner while Vishwas set up a sales and distribution network for a company named American Power Conversion (APC) which was entering India at that time. Once his partner was ready, he was ready to begin.

In 225 square feet of space in an outhouse of a Pune bungalow, Compulink came into being in January 1996. The two partners had clearly defined roles. Says Vishwas, 'While Uday looked into the technological side, I handled the sales, marketing and distribution.' Where did the funds come from? He responds, 'The initial funding came from me since I had saved up some money during my tenure in Dubai. I used part of it to buy a home, and the rest of it to set up the company.' When the two of them started out, all they knew was that they wanted to be in the IT industry and that they wanted to do something different after making a transition from being employees and turning into entrepreneurs.

They started with outsourced product development for foreign companies. They had to start with smaller clientele since getting the big players was obviously very difficult. Their first client was a Swiss company with which they had dealings for a long time. The problem with these smaller companies was that they wanted the best possible supply by spending as little as possible. So these companies had very high expectations from Compulink. He took it as a challenge and as he puts it, 'It kept us on our toes.' It was a booming business but then they hit a roadblock: the IT bubble burst. Many of these companies collapsed and backed out of the projects and there was no way for Compulink to pursue legal action in foreign jurisdictions.

Non-payment by clients led to a crisis as the company already had hired more than 50 employees in Pune by that time. 'Because of this all of us had to go without salaries for a few months,' Vishwas recalls. But, necessity being the mother of all inventions, they weathered through this tumultuous time by getting into product invention. They always had problems recruiting through top colleges in Pune, which made them recruit students from Kolhapur, Satara and Aurangabad. Only shortlisted candidates went through the grind of interviews and psychometric tests before being hired. Vishwas reflects, 'They had to undergo some training. But they were very intelligent individuals who delivered the goods and were assets to the company.'

Their first product was called HireByNet, an online recruitment tool. They exhibited their project in a Las Vegas convention, and to their surprise, got an offer for $200,000. They gleefully accepted it as a nice bargain. This sowed the seeds of their development in a new direction: Creating their own IP and products.

From 2001 to 2009, Compulink was known as a project management product company. It slowly started including high-profile clientele like Accenture, Wipro and Fujitsu who had the capacity of making products themselves. But as Vishwas puts it, 'It was like selling medical services to a doctor.' They relied on Compulink for the cross-industry experience, cost advantage and, therefore, had huge expectations of a superior product at a lesser price from Compulink. The company became one of the very few to generate the 100-crore revenue mark in software product licensing revenues. They initially managed to get venture capital funding and then took the company public on Indian bourses. In 2009, Vishwas made a decision to sell Compulink. 'It was time to make sure that the company merged with a bigger entity and attained higher goals.' They followed a proper process for exit and Compulink eventually merged with Glodyne, an e-governance company also listed in the Bombay Stock Exchange.

After such an illustrious career, it was time to give it back to the society. One thing that was always close to his heart was helping young entrepreneurs. That brought him closer to The Indus Entrepreneurs (TiE), a global organization that aids budding entrepreneurs. He is also the majority stakeholder in Lifeline Technologies, an IT product and support company;

Compulink Academy, a finishing school for engineering graduates headed by Compulink's co-founder Uday; and Artitude, a performing arts education venture. He is also an angel investor in Kapsica Media, a digital ad agency. 'At the moment, you can say that I am taking a sabbatical,' he says.

SUCCESS MANTRAS

'Young entrepreneurs need to be persistent. There will be a lot of naysayers and roadblocks along the way. If you give up, then you haven't tried enough.' He quotes Paulo Coelho, 'If you have a dream, stick to it, the universe will conspire to get to what you desire.'

Follow what the Nike advertisement says: Just do it.

PANKAJ KESWANI
Alufit India Pvt. Ltd

Pankaj Keswani heads Alufit, which is among the biggest names in the structural glazing business in India. When one views his stature, the story of his struggle is impossible to imagine.

༄

THE MAVERICK ENTREPRENEUR

Aravind Haridas and Divya Sharma

Whether you are at work at one of the towering office buildings or you are having fun shopping or catching a movie at one of the city's most happening malls, chances are that no matter where you are in Bangalore, you are in one of Pankaj Keswani's creations. The charming, middle-aged man has changed the way buildings of Bangalore look by covering them with gleaming glass façades. Founder of Alufit India Pvt. Ltd, which is one of the biggest names in the ₹2000-crore façade engineering industry in India, with an annual turnover touching ₹200 crore, Keswani has a story of his life and work which can give Bollywood a run for its money.

Based in Bangalore, we were scheduled to meet the man behind Alufit, one of the biggest names in the structural glazing business in the country. After having already put in an entire day at work, he is absolutely fresh at 7.30 in the evening. In no time he sits down with us, eager to share his life's story, the mug in his hand brimming with piping hot coffee. As the brave and fearless businessman recounted his riveting story, we sat, mesmerized, hanging on to every single word of his. The intrepid businessman sitting in front of us had experienced several highs and lows in his life. What we knew, then and there, was that narrating the story of his life won't be easy.

The magnitude of Pankaj's success stands in glaring contrast to the modest ambitions of his initial days at the Shriram Group. 'At that time, I used to say to myself that my aim was to make ₹30,000 a month when I retire,' he confesses with a smile.

Today, Pankaj's Alufit is one of the largest firms in India in the field of curtain walling. With an annual turnover of more than ₹100 crore, his earnings today have gone way beyond his initial modest ambitions. 'The aluminium/structural glazing market in the country would be about ₹2000 crore out of which more than a 1000 crore would fall into the unorganized sector. The business of structural glazing involves turnkey projects to clad buildings with glass and aluminium. When a structure is under construction, the client floats a tender. If we get the job, we design the system for the building; we source the material, fabricate and assemble it in our factory and ship it to the site, whether it is in Bangalore, Chennai, Pune, Trivandrum, Bhubaneswar or Delhi, where it is then installed on the building. A few prime examples of this are the IT campuses of Infosys, TCS, HCL and Wipro.''

'Currently we have about twenty projects going on at various stages—some at the design stage, some at execution and a few at handing over. These range from ₹10 crore to ₹60 crore with selected clients. The biggest of them is Tata Consultancy Services (TCS) with whom we are doing projects in excess of 75 crore,' he informs.

Pankaj Keswani was born to industrious Sindhi middle class parents without any business background. His father being a government employee and his mother a medical doctor, bringing up three kids in the best possible manner was a tough challenge.

Keswani's early life wasn't particularly eventful. Like many other youngsters of his time, he went on to do his B.Com. and chose Sydenham College situated close to his residence in Mumbai's Napean Sea Road.

He never thought of becoming an entrepreneur until he joined the Delhi-based Shriram Group as a management trainee. 'No thought of entrepreneurship had occurred to me earlier. But I did have an exposure to business in my extended family. I think seeing my cousins enjoying all the comforts of life made an impression on me, and I grew up wanting the same.'

'It is difficult when you are from a service background. I used to wear hand-me-downs from my brother and socks with a rubber band, and I had had enough of it. I didn't want my children to go through that. The only disagreements we had at home were related to money. So I realized how important money was. The only way I could sort out this problem was getting into a business.'

After finishing his MBA, Pankaj had the option of joining his brother's firm. However, he had his eyes set on the corporate world and joined the Shriram Group as a management trainee. But after working for a year, he realized that his hard work wasn't paying off. He then decided to leave his job and join his brother's company, which, by then, was well established. Although he was leaving a cushy and secure job, his parents were very happy that Pankaj had joined his brother. They hoped that theirs would be one big business family some day.

However, Pankaj's experience in his brother's company was shortlived. 'You kids won't realize it now, but personal and professional relationships are vastly different. While one can have a great equation in one's personal life, in business your thoughts, value systems and approaches can be so different that at times it makes it impossible to work together,' he says, adding, 'We were like chalk and cheese, what I called white he called black. So I thought when we were so distinct in our professional qualities and had strong individual traits why not preserve them and take our own paths? So I decided to quit and told my brother that I couldn't work with him anymore.'

The turmoil inside Pankaj's head is easy to imagine. 'I left my brother's factory at Mahalaxmi industrial estate, Lower Parel. It was 2.30 in the afternoon, and I was wondering what I would tell my parents. I boarded a train to Churchgate and went to Nariman Point, introspecting and asking myself what I really wanted from my life. I was 23 and I had left a cushy job thinking I would join my brother and build an empire. But now I had nothing in hand. I wondered about my options. I couldn't go back to a job because I did not want to go back to ₹1500 a month and also felt there was no long-term growth in that area. I had many friends in business—businesses like garments and plastics—and I wondered if I could try my hand at any of those. But then I realized that I knew nothing about these businesses and the only field I had any knowledge about was aluminium. The advantage of working in a small business was that I had seen every department of the business—planning, production, execution, client handling and marketing.

'The next question was where could I start the business. Though Mumbai was comfortable, I couldn't have started it in Mumbai as I would have been in direct competition with my brother which wouldn't have been fair to him as we lived in the same house and sat at the same dinner table. Hence I had to get out of Mumbai. The markets were very different then, Chennai was still Madras at that time and Bangalore still a pensioner's paradise. Things were all Mumbai-centric, but I had to take the hard decision of moving out of Mumbai so as not to step on my brother's toes.

'The first step after deciding to move out of Mumbai was to look for a place to set up my business. The option that came to my mind was Pune as I had lived here for two years while doing my MBA at Symbiosis. However, the IT revolution was yet to happen and Pune was a small place with not much activity. So I looked at other metros, Delhi, Kolkata, Chennai, Hyderabad and Bangalore.

'Calcutta, now Kolkata, was a dying city with no infrastructure, so it was out. Delhi was a great option as I spoke the languages, both Hindi and Punjabi. But I was a little wary of the people. *'Muh mein ram, ram, bagal mein chhuri'* sums up how I felt about them. They were so sweet to me that I thought they would kill me the next morning,' he carries on with his amazing story, 'I checked out Chennai but then I didn't speak the language. I boarded autos where drivers understood neither Hindi nor English. Here I was to revolutionize the way buildings looked and Chennai then had no sophistication of this kind on offer. Last on my "to-see" list was Bangalore. The place had a cosmopolitan touch. It had beautiful buildings, interesting architecture and the people were not so conservative. I met some architects and some more people and I felt comfortable. It felt a lot like Mumbai, plus the weather was something to die for.'

Each moment of his life was precious, and he knew it better than anyone else. 'I took up a small lodge for ₹20 per day and went across to meet architects. The professionals I met said they could give me business provided I was based out of there. One such architect's firm was Sanath Kumar and Associates, and I showed the architect my sections and samples. He said he was designing the Salgaocar Group's guesthouse and I could quote for it. I jumped at the offer. I was hungry for work. I wanted to settle down in Bangalore, and if they gave me work, I would have a reason to settle down there.'

The architect was impressed by Pankaj's passion. He smiled and said, 'I like your enthusiasm, but I am not the final authority. You will have to meet the client in Goa. How soon can you go?' He was elated at the chance of getting his first order and wasted no time thinking it over. 'So I took the next bus to Goa and reached Vasco at 9 a.m., rushed to meet the client at 10 o'clock.'

The Salgaocars wanted to replicate the windows they had at their Mumbai guesthouse. Pankaj was promised the contract provided he could do the job. 'Within two hours, I boarded a train to Mumbai and went straight to the house. I looked at the windows. I called them up and said yes, I could do it. They gave me an appointment ten days hence in Bangalore.'

Thus, one week after leaving his brother's company, he was back in Mumbai with a potential project in hand. 'I went home and told my parents that I was moving to Bangalore, that I wanted to find my own space without being a competition to Navin. At first thought, they thought that I was out of my mind to leave everything that was already set up. They felt I would be back to my senses soon.' However, he packed his bag and boarded a train to Bangalore to set up shop and stayed with Sudhir Hegde, a dear friend from his Sydenham days.

The deal was finally closed for a sum of ₹35000. Armed with an advance of ₹5000 from the client, Pankaj scouted around for capital from friends and family. Close friends, Suresh Rajani loaned him ₹5000, Rakesh Khandelwal loaned ₹6000 and his own brother gifted him ₹5000. Pankaj was given ₹1000 by his father while a wealthy uncle of his was his largest investor with ₹30,000 coming from him. Armed with this capital, he searched for a factory, and paid a sum of ₹30,000 in advance, promising to pay the balance later. Thus in the year 1984, at age twenty-four, with humble beginnings and unabashed ambitions, Pankaj Keswani started his entrepreneurial journey.

Today, Pankaj believes that time has vindicated his hasty decisions. 'You have to take some decisions in life. You have to hold the bull by its horns. You can't expect things to fall into your lap. I wanted to set up my business, I didn't do any SWOT analysis before setting it up. I just had to do it. I was just very young back then, and what could possibly go wrong? I only had to fend for myself and send some money back home. In my heart I knew what I was good at, which the competition didn't know as yet. By the time they would come up to speed, time would pass. I would have the first mover's advantage.'

While Pankaj was blessed with a bunch of well-wishers who helped him set up his business, his real pillar of support and greatest source of encouragement had always been his wife Vyjayanthi Keswani, who is now the Director of Finance at Alufit. She has started to help Pankaj out with his business recently but is a businesswoman in her own right. She used to work for Diners Club during his early start-up days, and then she quit work. For close to five years she was a full-time homemaker and then she went on to set up a company called Linani, an interior decorations/soft furnishings company.

His face lights up with a glow, and he sinks down in his

chair while indulging himself in the fond reminiscence of his initial days with her. 'I had a girlfriend who is now my wife. We used to stay in the same colony in Napean Sea Road in Mumbai. We started dating when we were 17 and I proposed to her a month after we met in a 106 BEST bus. She thought I was crazy, but eventually I won her over and we started dating.'

After the two of them got married, they started out life together in Bangalore in a small barsati on the first floor of a bungalow. 'When I was searching for houses all over Bangalore, I couldn't afford to spend more than ₹700 a month on a house, and all good houses were around ₹1200. So I settled for a barsati which suited my budget. Just before leaving for my wedding, in that one day I bought some utensils, a heater, a bucket and an immersion rod and two mattresses, all for some ₹300, and I had nothing else in the house.'

Fortunately for Pankaj, his business caught up quite fast in Bangalore and the initial teething troubles lasted only a year. 'My business changed fast and with some more loans from my uncle I expanded the business. I now had customers and I started returning money I had borrowed. I was pretty happy with what I was doing, and I had a passion for it. And as long as I had enough money to put gas in the car and food on the table, I was fine.'

From then on, Pankaj never had to look back, and money was never a criterion for him anymore. 'And in any case I was earning many more bucks than I would have in any other career and while my business was small then, the profits were quite high. Within two years I was earning around ₹50,000 per month as I was operating at 30 per cent margins. But now the situation is different especially after 2008–09 as the margins have dried out and we are currently operating at sub-10 per cent levels.'

After the initial euphoria of setting up, growth was not so fast during the latter years. Although Pankaj was able to repay his debt and break even under less than two years, the annual revenue of Alufit touched only ₹6 crore in 2000. This sluggishness in the growth made him a little restless. 'This was the time I was getting frustrated and planned to move into construction. I thought I had far more talent than to get stuck in a rut. I worked for 12–14 hours everyday and made only around 30 lakhs of profit while my other builder friends made 10 times the money for half the effort put in.'

'I thought I was just a sophisticated carpenter with an MBA degree and I was being under-utilized. I should get into something which has better growth and higher turnover. I knew I had more potential and I could do much more. I felt I could play a bigger role and that's why I wanted to get into construction, however, I was in a Catch-22 situation. I understood this line, got into it and built a business, it made no sense to leave it for something else.

'And then just when I was having thoughts of quitting, structural glazing came in and the whole market changed. From doing regular doors and windows, we started enveloping and cladding entire buildings. From 2000 to 2001 we grew from ₹6 crore to ₹10 crore and through 2002 to 2003 we grew from ₹14 crore to ₹23 crore.' The advent of the IT and ITES revolution in India accelerated the growth of Alufit. And Bangalore evolving as the most preferred city for huge IT parks and modern glazed buildings furthered his cause tremendously. 'I had never paid cognizance to the fact that I had done something interesting and unique for the industry—it just felt like another day at the office. Fear was an unknown thing.'

The real turning point in Pankaj's entrepreneurial journey came about in 2008–09. 'I had these 25 glorious years in the industry and was having a brilliant run. I had built everything from scratch, and I thought I had the midas touch. So I set up an extrusion plant.' He explains what it meant for his business. 'I was consuming quite a fair amount of aluminium for my own business. So I thought it was a wise decision, considering at least 15 per cent of my production would be used by me and the rest I could offload in the open market. Till then, my business required me to source extruded sections from Hindalco, Jindal, etc., fabricate and assemble it and then put it together for my clients. I decided to now get into production—buying ingots/billets and form them into extruded sections and then continue with the fabrication and assembly. I decided to set up a plant, a new facility, everything. This was a capital-intensive venture and quite unlike my other business where all I had to do was put in a crore or roundabouts in terms of machinery and in turn I could do a business of a 100 crore annually.' This was an audacious venture. And like most entrepreneurs, he was confident to the core. 'Here I was putting in ₹70–75 crore into the project and I didn't think much about it. I didn't even bother to do a project report.'

'I just thought I knew aluminium and I had been in this business for 25 years—I could do it. I didn't really study whether there was a margin or about the production costs and what would be the payback period. I just felt that if Jindal could do 4000 tonnes; Bhoruka could do a 1000 tonnes, I could surely do 500 tonnes a month.'

Pankaj felt that with years of hard work and dedication he

has built a name for himself in his industry, and if he were to venture into manufacturing, he would leave no stone unturned to ensure that his was the best plant. 'I went about building India's best plant. I felt that when I built my plant, it had to be better than Jindal, better than anyone in the industry.'

Pankaj started out with a plan of building the plant in early 2007 but was in for a rude shock when all of a sudden came the global meltdown of 2008 which threw everything out of gear. Even Pankaj wasn't spared the heat and he had to face trying times. Those were the times that tested his faith in himself, his will to fight and his resolve to stay put.

'I had started off with a plan to set up the extrusion facility when the market was really looking up and the dollar was at ₹38–40 levels. When the machinery finally arrived in, November 2008 it was 50 bucks to a dollar. By which time the Lehman Bros had collapsed and the markets were in recession. When we finally started commercial operations it was February 2009, and recession had hit its peak. I had invested around ₹15 crore. So I ended up borrowing around 60 crore. At that time I had rejected the bank's offer for a holiday period, because the interest would obviously keep mounting.'

'I had to pay them ₹50 lakhs a month towards the principal and ₹60 lakhs interest. By the time production started in 2009 I had to pay 1.1 crores to the bank every month. I thought my own business of fabrication would bring in a crore of surplus every month. I could use this money to pay the bank. So I would see my plant through. Logically it made sense. I had never thought that I would hit recession and this would probably be the worst period in my life. I went back to the banks for a debt restructure and they refused.

'In the meantime, my fabrication business had collapsed, the markets were in recession and no one wanted to build. There were no customers, my collections dried up but my obligation to the bank continued every morning. To add to my woes, I didn't have to deal just with repayment, there are teething problems in a new plant and it needs a lot of hand holding. Every month I hence had an out flow of close to ₹1.5 crore, my inflows had practically dried up and my working capital started taking a hit. So I sold the only property that was not mortgaged and paid ₹25 to the bank. This helped me buy time with the banks for a year.

'With this done, my interest burden came down to ₹35 lakhs every month, and also I did not have the burden of paying them 1.5 crore every quarter as principal. As far as the sold property was concerned, I felt that in any case the money had come from the business. Yes, I had a property to show for it, but the business built it and now the business needed it. So when the company is in a crisis, the first thing one should do is to sell off what is not required.'

This was the time when Pankaj realized how highly leveraged he really was. On a ₹110-crore turnover he had a loan of ₹60 crore. With markets looking down and customers not paying up, Alufit valuations went down. 'I was quite helpless. I spoke to investment bankers and they all said I should bide my time for another six months. So the moment things started looking up in 2010 I decided I needed someone to take up about 30 per cent stake. I figured that if I would be valued at ₹200 crore, by giving up 30 per cent stake I could get in ₹60 crore in return. I then would be able to pay off the banks their 35 crore and still have 20 crore left.'

It was a harrowing time for him, the worst he ever faced in his business. 'There were times when during that period, I would take a flight and wish the plane would crash. When there was turbulence and everybody on the flight was looking at each other with fear in their eyes, I'd be happy and expectant. I wouldn't have to get down, call my suppliers and answer the banks.'

'Everybody knew the kind of trouble I was in because I was not able to meet my obligations.' At this point Pankaj's eyes welled up and his voice cracked under the weight of his emotions 'For 25 years I paid my salaries on the seventh of every month. That was our date. I still remember that day in November 2009 I couldn't muster up the money and that day I cried.'

Around the same time, the SAPA group from Sweden approached Pankaj for buying some extrusions. They visited his spanking new state-of-the-art plant at Kuppam, in Chittoor district, Andhra Pradesh, which is a two-hour drive from Bangalore. Pankaj immediately sensed an opportunity. 'I had the best equipment, the best plant, and they were quite impressed with it. So I pitched to them that being global number one, why don't they join hands with me instead of buying from me?'

Two weeks later, a meeting took place between the Alufit officials and the merger and acquisitions team of the SAPA group, which had come down from Norway to visit the plant. They came down to India again in August 2010 for negotiations. 'I offered them a 30 per cent stake in my extrusion business, not my whole business. I figured that if they valued the extrusions for ₹100 crore, that would give me ₹30 crore, I would then be able to reasonably stabilize my business. They, on the other hand, were not interested in a minority stake and replied that they wouldn't be interested in any stake that is less than 51 per cent. Multiple rounds of discussions followed and the SAPA group were warming up to the offer slowly—they upped their offer to 25 million dollars from the initial 20 million. The turning point happened when they made an offer for a complete buyout and asked Pankaj to name a price.

The story takes an interesting turn from here and this is where we can see the real maverick in Pankaj Keswani. 'I could have taken the easy way out. I could have walked with 25 million for it was more than what I had bargained for—my neck was on the line, my business was bust and I was one step away from bankruptcy. But I had not built this business just to sell it. I was doing this deal because I had to get out of a spot. So I told my team that I've decided—it is going to be 35 million.' His team of advisors were sceptical. 'It is going to look silly; you are going to end up looking preposterous.' Pankaj, on the other hand, decided to follow his heart. 'I said no, I think I'll do it, I can pull it off.'

Moreover, selling off the factory was not an easy decision for Pankaj 'It is like only a mother knows what goes on in her for nine months but nobody else does. They didn't know what I had been through to build that plant. I built that plant from scratch. I bought barren land and filled it up and I built the plant there.'

He wasn't too sure that he wanted to sell 100 per cent of the plant. But at the same time, he was also fully aware of the glaring fact that he did not have much of an opportunity to negotiate, because he was in desperate need of someone to bail him out. In his own words, 'No one knew how badly I was in debt, right? They just saw my flashy cars, my Benz, my BMW—

but they didn't know how much I was struggling inside since the cars were bought during the good times. I just happened to fall into bad times because of one poor decision.' At the same time, Pankaj was shrewd enough to realize one thing. 'While I was anxious to get out of trouble, they were twice as anxious to get into India and I used that knowledge to my advantage.' Backed with this, he started the second round of negotiations and by then he was quite confident of what he wanted. 'Across me on the negotiation table was the President M&A of SAPA Svein Tore Holsether who later on went on to become their CEO. We were about to break for lunch and I asked my team and his to leave the room, give us 20 minutes together.

While Pankaj recreated the part in front of us, I couldn't help but think that this could have as well been a scene from one of those Hollywood thrillers. 'I told Svein, "it's you and me who have to take the final call, and I am not going to sell this plant for less than 31 million. It's 31 million or it's not going to work."' Svein was taken by surprise at the new turn of events and he was quite forthright in his reply. 'I have a mandate of 30 million but, if you want 31 million, you would have to wait for a week, as I have to put this proposal up in front of our board, it could then go either way—either they'll say yes or they might drop the idea altogether of buying the plant.'

It was just a million, and anybody else would have closed the deal and shaken hands with that man right there, but not Pankaj. 'I figured that if I have to go down, it will not be without a fight. At 30 million, it was still a damn good deal for me, but then as they say, when you are a gambler, go for the jugular. Like I said earlier, I was not happy selling the plant. I was only doing it because I was in a crisis. If I had to bow out, I was going to go with my head held high.' And then in a week's time, Svein had the board's approval, finally closing the deal in May 2011 after due diligence and other formalities.

It was his day, and like a phoenix that rises from its ashes, Pankaj Keswani emerged stronger and, not to mention, wealthier by a few million dollars after the ravages of recession. 'I still remember the first thing that I did when this deal just got over.' He sent a message to his dear friends, few clients and customers saying—'Sir, this is debt-free Keswani reporting.'

When he was going through the crisis, he did lose some business as his focus was diverted initially towards setting up the plant and later on, towards trying to turn it around. 'The moment we sold the extrusion business, my clients welcomed me back with open arms and within six months we picked up more than ₹150 crore of work while the whole of last year we had done just about ₹100 crore.'

One obvious question that would spring to anyone's mind after listening to this compelling personal narrative would be his source of motivation during the difficult times. 'I had a great obligation to my staff and my workers. I thought they had done no wrong, no harm to be in the position they were in. By then we were a family of about 700–800 people. There was my extrusion team, my fabrication team and I had contractors and sub-contractors—all put together, some 800 families depended on me for their livelihood and I couldn't have gone down overnight. I had learn how to swim with the sharks. If things hadn't worked out with SAPA, I would have looked elsewhere. But then you can't expect things to happen by sitting at one place. You have to take a chance and you have to go for it, that is what business is all about'.

An entrepreneur, in essence, is an incurable optimist and Pankaj is no exception to the rule. 'They say every cloud has a silver lining and I knew that my time was just around the corner. One has to visualize to see the light at the end of the tunnel but for that one has to believe in oneself. I don't think there is anything more to it. And if you don't believe in yourself, you can't expect others to believe in you. When I would walk into my office in the morning, no matter how bad the previous night was, I'd walk in with a big smile, feeling all fresh. I had to be the leader, and I had to be the source of inspiration. While I could cry in my privacy, I couldn't do that in front of my people for that would crush them. Through the crisis, my people stood by me and they did not ask for an increment.'

With the worst being over, Pankaj is very optimistic about the year ahead. 'Currently our business is at around ₹120 crore and I have a lot of optimism for the following year. My 2013–14 order books would be opening at about ₹250 crore. And if I open at that level, I can look to do ₹200 crores by March 2014.'

SUCCESS MANTRAS

'Learn from the tough times.

'I thought I never ever deserved to get into this spot I found myself in post the recession of 2008. I used to question why this was happening to me? But then I would rationalize—"I had a glorious run for 25 years and I never questioned it, why am I crying now? Let it be, this too, shall pass."

'And this is important for you kids. As you grow up, there will always be people who armchair critics, always telling you what you shouldn't do and what you should have done. They are all there to advise you when it doesn't go right. But no one is there to tell you when you are actually doing your business well. The moment something goes right, they attribute it to luck. They say you were at the right place at the right time. No one will tell you that you took the right decision, worked hard and you built it.'

QUALITIES OF AN ENTREPRENEUR

'As an entrepreneur what you really have to have is a strong self-belief. You have got to believe you have it in you to set up a company, you can turn it around, you can build a business and you can create a fortune. The other side of it is—it's all very good for you to believe in it but, you have to work for it. You can't just desire. Entrepreneurs can't just be made with self-belief alone. I think it takes a lot of never-ending passion, hard work, persistence and determination. Nothing is made overnight and you have to earn every cent and every penny.

'Additionally, you need to have the right approach, you need to know how to interact with people—it's a combination of many factors. That's because a customer is not always looking for the lowest price. They are also looking for delivery, quality and comfort in their dealing. If your total package is better than your competitors, that is what matters.'

MEANING OF SUCCESS

'Nothing lasts for ever. When you go up the ladder, the people you meet on your way up are the same ones you meet on your way down. If you kick people on your way up, you can be dead sure they will trip you on your way down, so on your journey up the ladder always be modest, understanding and be reasonable. Even today, I really don't distinguish between my driver, office boy and other members of the staff. In fact, we all wear the same shirt, the one that I am wearing right now.' And so said he signs off, ready to face whatever tomorrow may bring.

PRADEEP GIDWANI
The Pint Room

Pradeep Gidwani worked with several start-ups in the alcoholic beverages industry. But he is best known for being the mind behind The Pint Room, a beer café chain.

ᗰ

PITCHER PERFECT

Surya Vardhan Azad and Sofia Parveen

Pradeep Gidwani is a stalwart in the Indian alcoholic beverages industry. We met him at the Pune outlet of The Pint Room, a unique café which serves different types of beer. Since the time Pradeep launched The Pint Room in December 2010 in Delhi, the chain has been a huge success in many major cities.

In his characteristic informal style, he walks us through the twists and turns in his corporate life that had him heading companies such as Foster's, Red Bull, Carlsberg, Moët Hennessy and Diageo's Scotch whiskies. It's a fascinating story, one that involves associations with six start-ups in India. However, Pradeep didn't experience his eureka moment at The Pint Room. That happened elsewhere, almost one decade earlier.

As a youngster, Pradeep frequently relocated from one city to another. His father was with the Indian Forest Services, which entailed transfers every couple of years. In fact, he changed 10 schools in 10 years! It would have been a frustrating situation for anyone, but not him. 'Ten schools in 10 years was actually fun, and when I look back, I see I have got friends in almost every city,' he grins.

He attributes his success to the exposure he gained in the process of changing cities. 'I lived in different places like

Dehradun, Ooty, Goa, Coimbatore. Because of changing so many places in my early years, I learnt to adapt along with learning the ability to make friends wherever I went. I think that is critical to any person's success.'

He did well in school up until the 10th standard. But, studies and school took a backseat when he moved to Goa where he 'ended up doing nothing but partying' as he admits with a smile. He ended up botching up his scores, as a result of which getting admission in a Medicine or Engineering course was out of question. After completing his BSc in Mathematics from Nowrosjee Wadia College in Pune, he gravitated towards an MBA degree.

What made him opt for an MBA? He says, 'MBA as a career platform was evolving at the time. I was very excited about it. I spent a lot of time reading management books, autobiographies and business magazines. That's when my interest in MBA piqued me and I decided to go for it, and I got admission into SIBM Pune.'

Pradeep's first job after he earned an MBA degree was with Hindustan Lever's Brooke Bond. After selling tea, coffee and spices during his two-year tenure as a young employee with the company, he moved into advertising. He took up a job with Everest Advertising, then a Saatchi & Saatchi Group company. 'There I learned about media planning, creative, making ad spots, radio spots, artworks and accounts. I worked on UB Group (Herbetsons), Swiss Air, Tips & Toes cosmetics, Mahindra Tractors, Tortoise Mosquito coils—a fairly interesting mix of products.'

It was there that he had his first tryst with the industry of alcoholic beverages. 'At Everest I was handling Herbertson's range of alcoholic products. I didn't ask for it, but I was very happy at getting it. The United Breweries (UB) Group at the time was setting up a joint venture with United Distillers Plc. (now Diageo) and I was offered an option to join them in the sales and marketing function—I took it up.'

United Distillers India Ltd—a joint venture company set up by United Distillers Plc. and the UB Group—also gave him his first taste of being involved with a start-up. 'I was one of the first few employees to join the company and my job was to handle sales and marketing.' He rose through the ranks fairly quickly, and in 1997 he was promoted to the position of General Manager (South Asia), United Distillers Plc.

Later that year, Foster's was setting up base in India, and offered him the big ticket: the role of Vice President, Sales and Marketing. Given his penchant for start-ups, he took it up gladly. However, it wasn't all smooth sailing. 'When Foster's came to India, it was a large company globally. But in China they hadn't done very well. So, in spite of being a huge company, they decided to not invest too much money in India. India was much like an abandoned baby. At that time I remember thinking, "Where have I joined up?"

'In hindsight, it was one of the most enriching experiences, because I was pretty much left to fend for myself; I had been thrown in at the deep end of the pool. We had no resources, no money, nothing. So you weren't an MNC which had a parent company which wrote cheques for you. We had to earn our own money. It was very difficult, but we began building the company with a lot of passion.'

Foster's under Pradeep was an exciting place to be in. 'Ninety-nine per cent of beer in India was being sold in 650 ml bottles. Foster's launched the 330 ml bottle even though two others had tried and failed. It became highly successful.' The company thrived under him. It became a household name after the 'Australian for beer' campaign, and captured 25 per cent market share in Maharashtra within the first two years of its launch. India had become Foster's third largest market in the world, a huge achievement in a short period.

Pradeep left Foster's for a brief period and enjoyed a short stint with Louis Vuitton Mët Hennessy as Chief Representative, where he launched the Hennessy Cognac, Mët & Chandon champagne and is largely credited for introducing such fine products on the Indian scene. He re-joined Foster's as Managing Director in May 2000.

His accomplishments began to be recognized and acknowledged. In September 2002, he was on the cover of the leading business magazine: *Business Today*. The cover story was titled, 'The Hottest Young Executives of India: India's 25 Rising Stars'. 'That was something that gave me a big high.'

Things were going smoothly when Pradeep received a bolt from the blue. Foster's was exiting the beer business globally. 'I had to go to Singapore and make presentations to potential buyers. I was there selling the baby I'd brought up with my own hands.'

Every cloud has a silver lining. 'Through the course of those presentations, the price of Foster's India just kept going up and up. The Indian business of Foster's was one of the most wanted, and we took pride in the fact that it was due to our hard work. That business eventually sold for a fortune of $120 million!'

The entrepreneur within Pradeep saw the opportunity

beginning to present itself. 'We had built that business with our bare hands; we had no tools. I then saw how that company was being valued. And that's when I thought that it had been long since I had been building businesses for others, and that I should now be building something for myself. After that it was only a matter of time before I started on my own.'

The switch didn't happen overnight. Following the sale of Foster's in 2006, he went on to head Red Bull and launched it across Asia. He later returned to India to launch Carlsberg, another start-up. He quit Carlsberg in January 2010 with the aim of doing something of his own.

THE RIGHT IDEA

Familiar with alcoholic beverages largely because of the seven years he had spent in Goa, Pradeep thought of launching a beer café. He explains, 'I have always thought that beer is a casual drink, something people can have a conversation over, just like coffee, as opposed to drinks like whisky which are more serious.'

'So I thought about the kind of places where people could meet and have conversations. So if you need to meet somebody, where would you go? A coffee shop? I think that's very boring. So if not a coffee shop you'd end up going to a bar. A bar is noisy—it's crowded, it's loud, and it's dark. So the other option would be to meet somebody at a local city club, but many people don't have access to clubs. So, why not a beer café?'

'That's when I said to myself, "let me create something which gives you the same coffee-shop-like relaxed experience but with beer." So you come here at any time to catch up with your friends, family or mates from work, and just enjoy your beer and relax.' What made him optimistic about his idea was that he had experienced the coffee revolution in India. 'When it actually began; no one believed that coffee shops would succeed in a country where tea was the big drink. Thus was born the idea of a beer café where beer would be sold just as coffee is sold in coffee shops.'

The concept of a brightly lit ambience at The Pint Room with soft music humming in the background was linked to his idea. 'I wanted to take beer out of that "somewhat-taboo" alcohol space and put it in that "meeting place" space just like coffee shops—where people could meet without thinking they were doing something "wrong". I wanted the place to have a very relaxed and casual look and feel.'

Every person who starts out with a new entrepreneurial idea faces challenges, and so did Pradeep. He admits, 'Challenges are many. From government regulations, operating environments, lack of funding, small team and resources, there is a lot to do. One has to be able to think the big picture as well as the micro-detail.' Since he had decided to enter the business of selling alcoholic beverages, he had to deal with a lot more. 'India is a tough operating environment, particularly in an industry where alcoholic beverages are a part of restrictions. This makes operating difficult since one is bound by numerous rules and regulations. One slip up and your business can be shut for any whimsical reason.'

The journey from an idea as a dream to its actual fruition wasn't free from roadblocks, which were regulatory in nature. Since setting up a café involves getting numerous licences from various authorities and this varies state by state, this process could be time-consuming and frustrating. As he took one step at a time, he learnt what it actually meant. He adds, 'It takes time for people to understand the concept. Initially, people thought that The Pint Room was a bar. Now they understand that The Pint Room is a simple, down-to-earth meet-up place over beers.'

The Pint Room opened in December 2010 and received a phenomenal response—in the middle of a chilly winter! 'It was crazy. We hadn't anticipated that kind of a crowd. I was behind the bar serving drinks myself and even washing glasses. It was great fun seeing the crowd coming in, and us hitting the numbers that we did. It meant the idea was being well received and that the "numbers" were working.' The Pint Room ended up selling 2,700 litres of beer that month. 'Those were very good volumes. And that increased more than two-fold over the next few months.'

So what lies ahead for Pradeep and The Pint Room? 'Our vision is very clear—I want us to be the "Starbucks of beer". If you look at the time Howard Schultz founded Starbucks, there was hardly any culture around coffee in the manner that it is now. That's when he created the concept of coffee shops. It has since evolved and now there are many following in the footsteps of Starbucks.'

Today The Pint Room operates eight cafés across India in Delhi, Gurgaon, Chandigarh, Mumbai, Pune and Bangalore. Two more will be launched in Delhi shortly, a good enough indication of an unusual and inspiring success story. The Pint Room outlets in Delhi NCR and Chandigarh offer five beers on tap. Besides, there are 35–50 brands of bottled beers in different outlets, depending on availability. He talks about his role, 'As a start-up, I have initially been involved in almost all aspects of the business. Today, we employ over 100 people in the company and the work is divided between them. My role is to be the coach to each of my team members.'

True to his hands-on style, Pradeep has put in a lot of elbow grease. 'We haven't used consultants, advertising agencies or marketing gurus to tell us what this is about. We were very clear about what we wanted it to be. I also designed this place myself without using an architect. I even decided on things like plumbing. I know about every single thing here, even things like the number of beer bottles lying in the fridge at any point of time.'

'I'm happy that we are changing the way people look at alcohol, and creating a completely new culture. So, if you are actually hanging around here on a weekend, and you look at the profile of the people coming in, it's actually quite interesting. You don't get the traditional bar crowd as it's bright and open instead of being dark and dingy—the place looks like a coffee shop. We even have grandparents coming here, and families coming with their kids. We also get women consumers coming in on their own as late as 10 p.m. I think this cultural shift in space for beer is needed in India.'

Moreover, the place is constantly evolving. 'As you grow, the business also keeps evolving with the help of new ideas. As the idea develops, you see the potential in it to be something more. I feel that's critical to any business. Starbucks started the coffee shop trend, and there are hundreds of them now around the world. I have started with a concept, and if this continues to work, there will be other beer cafés coming up pretty soon, which is why this place needs to evolve, and become that something more.'

When Pradeep had started out, people around him had

expressed their apprehensions. 'I was told that this idea wouldn't work because the per capita consumption of beer in India was extremely low at 1.5 litres as compared to 160 in the Czech Republic or 130 in Germany.' Instead of getting discouraged, he looked at that figure as an opportunity. 'I said "Wow! Look at the amount of beer we can have India drinking!"'

And that's exactly what Pradeep is doing—a pint at a time.

SUCCESS MANTRAS

'As you grow, the business also keeps evolving with the help of new ideas. As the idea develops, you see the potential in it to be something more. I feel that's critical to any business.'

SUJATA KHANNA
Career Forum and Calibre Mindware

Sujata Khanna set up Career Forum for training MBA aspirants. Today, she heads Calibre Mindware, an ambitious venture that has penetrated international markets through offshore software product development.

ဢ

TIME TO MOVE ON

Niket Khaitan and Sahil Rohmetra

Thinking ahead of the times is the easiest way to success, but that's easier said than done. Meet Sujata Khanna, the founder of Career Forum and Calibre Mindware. She envisioned the pan-India institute Career Forum when MBA prep was a thing unheard of, and has now staked on emerging technologies through Calibre Mindware, an offshore software product development business venture.

'There has never been a better time to be an Indian entrepreneur than now' are the words she starts her interview with. Optimistic, considering the dynamism in the modern-day environment, this lady with distinctive ideas has delivered results that endorse her thoughts.

Pune-bred Sujata did her schooling at St Joseph's High School. Throughout her school days, she was a bright student, and particularly excelled in English and Mathematics. She graduated from Fergusson College with a major in Chemistry in 1984. During her college days, she actively pursued extracurricular activities like mountaineering, badminton and swimming. She excelled in the National Cadet Corps (NCC), reaching the rank of Under-officer. Along with all this, she also nurtured her passion for reading and writing. After she completed her graduation, she, like many other youngsters, was confronted with the same question. 'Why MBA?' Sujata replies, 'I didn't want to become a researcher in the corner of a lab. So an MS was out of the question. Just then someone told me of a new course called MBA and it sounded exciting. I took it up.'

Her MBA at SIBM Pune was the hectic, fun-filled learning experience that it is typically is known for. Having been a good student throughout, she didn't have a problem securing a job as a management trainee at the then new and growing HCL Technologies. Her job was to sell personal computers to other businesses at a whopping ₹ three lakhs per machine. It included everything from cold calling to following up to closing the deal. Computers were not available at retail outlets those days. It was hard work, and many a time she came across clients who were surprised when they found out that a woman was selling them computers. She describes her job as the 'greatest learning experience of my life, which helped me immensely when I finally decided to start my own business.'

'What was great about the job was the amount of time my mentor spent with me discussing each client. We would conduct a complete transactional analysis of the client and formulate the best way to negotiate, in order to ensure the deal was ours. This is where most of the learning happened. It taught me how to read people, how to prepare thoroughly for meetings in advance, how to close deals and, most importantly, how to sell my personality. This experience was invaluable, both when I switched jobs and when I started Career Forum.'

Then came, what we believe was the turning point of her career. She was offered a job at a smaller company, Sara Electronics, which paid her much more to take more responsibility. She was already being paid a 'princely sum' of

₹1800 per month at HCL. Sara more than doubled it, with a salary of ₹4000 per month, along with a much better designation. So, after having worked for about a year at HCL, she took the bait and jumped ship.

Her new job was nothing like her old one. Here, she didn't have erudite mentors watching over her, helping her correct her mistakes and gently nudging her in the right direction. The job here was to set base for the entry of Sara into the Pune–Pimpri–Chinchwad region. She had to set up the office from scratch, put together a team, start sales and compete with the big-wigs who were already well established. And being the true manager she is, she excelled in all areas.

In about nine months she had achieved what she had set out for. It necessitated diligence on her part, but she was no quitter. What is more important is what happened next. The realization that she had been working as an entrepreneur, but being paid as an employee, dawned upon her. She always knew that she didn't want to work for someone else forever. The Sara episode gave her the much needed experience and confidence to take the plunge. The job was her much needed epiphany.

'The question now was "what next". I always knew that I wanted to do something on my own. Now I had the confidence and experience from my work at Sara. Having done my MBA at a time when the course was just beginning to gain popularity, with just 180 MBA seats in all of Pune, and about 3000 applicants vying for them, it struck me that there was no training institute to guide or prepare MBA aspirants. I knew there was a latent demand for this kind of training, which would help increase one's chances of making it to one's dream B-school. It was the most logical next step for me. I had been there, done that and now I would show others how they could do it too. The best part about starting a training centre is that there is very little scope or need for compromising on one's morals, and this is what sealed the deal for me.'

'So I started off the old-school way. I leased out a classroom, bought some ad space in a local newspaper to publicize this new offering and waited for my first student. And waited. And waited a little more. My family's support during such uncertain times helped me a lot. I waited so long, that I was convinced no one would turn up. One day I took my baby along with me to office and voila, I had three customers on the same day. Maybe my baby was my lucky charm. It was about a month until I had a set of seven students that I could call a "batch". A month may not sound like a lot to most people but, trust me, when you have quit your well-paying job and have invested money in a business, a month of waiting seems like it's much more.'

'I started Career Forum with the first batch of seven students. We were a very tight-knit group and that batch performed well. By the end of the first year, I had enough students to recover my initial investment, which was good news.'

'One of the hallmarks of Career Forum,' says Sujata, 'is that I always wanted it to be a professionally run institute. Everything was structured. We pioneered the distribution of printed learning worksheets and study material to our students. Even when I had just started off and was the only teacher, I ensured that the course followed a strict structure. This obviously paid off.'

'With time I started comprehending the MBA prep market better. I was able to apply the marketing concepts of segmentation and positioning to my business and develop products for all types of students. For example, a student may not feel the need for classroom teaching but may need the course material and the test series. I had an offering for everyone. No matter what kind of student you are, in today's competitive environment you need to have some kind of contact with a training institute and I had a product for every kind of student.'

Career Forum went on to become the runaway success we all know it to be. 'With success came growth and for the first time we moved outside Pune, to Bangalore. Next was Mumbai. I knew that the core offering of Career Forum was its quality teaching and we didn't want it to get diluted. I maintained a very strict hiring standard, which was followed by rigorous orientation and training. I never hired local teachers for the convenience they offered,' she says. 'Instead, we recruited the best from where we got them and sent them to the cities where we needed them. It was an added cost no doubt, but when you want to standardize teaching quality like a McDonald's burger, no price is high enough. There was a point when we had guesthouses in Pune, Bangalore, Mumbai, Chennai, Hyderabad, and Delhi. None of our teachers went home after class.'

Another reason for the company's success was pioneering the usage of technology in education. Career Forum developed its own cutting edge Enterprise Resource Planning (ERP) solutions to manage its vast number of students and multiplying branches. It also developed testing and assessment platforms and offered online products long before online testing became a norm in the MBA entrance space. By 2004, Career Forum had 13 company-owned centres in six cities. By 2005, the demand had grown considerably and it seemed that a franchise-based model was the best way forward. With franchises came unimaginable growth, and by 2008, Career Forum had 63 centres across the length and breadth of the country.

CALIBRE MINDWARE

An ERP software is a suite of integrated applications for management of a business. Career Forum's ERP provided an integrated real-time view to its core business processes, using common databases. The ERP facilitated information flow between all the following business functions, and managed connections to outside stakeholders.

- Accounting and costing
- Course planning
- Batch planning and scheduling
- Faculty allocation
- Lecture tracking and feedback
- Attendance management
- Inventory management
- Marketing, sales and distribution
- Shipping and payment
- Franchise management
- Testing and assessment
- Web-based student interface

Some time back in 2005, Career Forum was approached by an educational institute to set up a complete ERP backbone for them, just like the one used by Career Forum. Now, setting up ERP backbones for other institutes was as core a business for them as running a restaurant is for Sachin Tendulkar. Nonetheless, they went ahead and did the job. The client loved it, and, before they knew it, Career Forum had landed a few more of these jobs. 'Suddenly, this seemed like a nice business and we founded a separate entity in the software development space,' says Sujata.

The in-house software development division, now branded Calibre®, was made into an independent profit centre. It offered complete software solutions to schools, colleges and universities across the country.

In 2008, Calibre® was spun off as a separate company, Calibre Mindware, with a mandate to foray into emerging technologies and penetrate foreign markets through offshore product development.

TIME TO MOVE ON

Sujata says, Every business sees cycles; you can't expect the same every time you keep growing. There are ups and downs. Successful entrepreneurs are those who know how to adapt with the times and move in the right direction. That is what separates the true entrepreneurs from the emotional ones.'

The recession that started in 2008 and continued for a few years saw the fortunes of Career Forum decline. The infrastructure that was geared up to service the vast multitude of students was servicing 40 per cent of its capacity by 2010. 'However,' says Sujata, 'Calibre Mindware had picked up steam, and we decided to focus more on exploiting the business potential of the software entity.' In 2013, after reigning successfully for over 20 years, the Career Forum brand was sold.

Calibre Mindware, meanwhile, is growing at a fast pace. It has forayed into international markets with a wide range of offerings that include the following.

- Global payments software for banking and finance
- Web-user interfaces and applications
- Mobile applications
- Educational enterprise business solutions
- Testing and assessment services
- Legacy systems upgrade and maintenance

Sujata is looking forward to an exciting phase in this company.

It has been a fantastic run for Sujata. She confides that entrepreneurship helped her move beyond the glass ceiling women face. Traditional barriers facing women never came her way. As far as environmental challenges go, well, there were the standard ones that all entrepreneurs face, but she says, nothing can be daunting when one's personal environment is strong.

'I have been lucky to have an extremely supportive family. My husband of 26 years has also had an enormous impact on my life. It was in our first jobs that we met and realized an amazing connection. We both strive to excel in whatever we do, but we help each other strive for new heights. He is my biggest fan and likewise, I am his. We constantly help each other as a two-way sounding board for ideas. I am privileged that my spouse is also my best friend.'

About two hours of time spent with Sujata has changed how we view the field of entrepreneurship. From the earlier risky option, it now seems adventurous. The stakes are high, but it offers a challenge like no other. Sujata Khanna seems to relish such an adrenaline rush. A lady who seems to have an inexhaustible source of energy, she enjoys every bit of the challenges she faces at work every day. Then again, not everybody can be a successful entrepreneur. They all say, 'pause, realize your inherent needs and then proceed towards success'. To those of us blindly jumping into the corporate bandwagon, Sujata surely epitomizes the qualities of a truly ambitious entrepreneur who we can all aspire to emulate.

SUCCESS MANTRAS

About her success, Sujata says, 'My twin goals at all times are self actualization and emotional fulfilment. Now, these don't just chance one's way; one must passionately, actively solicit them. My radar is actively tuned to any signals that show I am straying away from my goals.' In achieving these goals, she uses her four-point mantra: creativity, adaptability, collaboration and optimism.

'I believe that creativity is the epicentre of growth. I like to interact with creative people and foster creation, and that is probably what keeps me excited about what I do.

'The environment around oneself changes very fast—technology, trends, expectations, everything. I believe that I must stay abreast or I will lag behind. I believe that one must take responsibility for one's growth; one can never stop learning, and if one is not up-to-date, one will miss the bus. Hence, I try to create a learning environment around me.

'To a certain extent, I know my strengths; and I know my weaknesses better. I rely on people who complement me and I like to work with people I can respect and trust. I believe in building pillars of strength around me, hence, I am willing to go the extra mile for them.

'I believe that every problem has a solution; it's only a matter of time when you find it, if only you keep trying. I am an eternal optimist; nothing can be that bad simply if you are alive.'

DR YOGESH P. JADHAV AND NAVAL TOSHNIWAL
94.3 Tomato FM

Yogesh Jadhav and Naval Toshniwal believed that the radio could do magic. Working as a team, they have proved they were right with Radio Tomato (94.3 FM), a huge success story in Kolhapur and surrounding areas, and their experiment with a completely different format called 'APLA FM 91.9 (Our FM)'.

RIDING THE AIRWAVES

Karan Shah and Mukesh Pareek

The Pune office of Pudhari Publications was the setting for our meeting with Yogesh Jadhav, the young scion of Kolhapur's Jadhav family that boasts of freedom fighters who worked closely with the likes of Mahatma Gandhi and Pandit Nehru. We were soon joined by his brother-in-arms, Naval Toshniwal. It is said that on the torturous path of entrepreneurship, the company of a fellow traveller can go a long way towards ensuring success and this is a conviction that Yogesh had right from the beginning of his own entrepreneurial journey. He met Naval Toshniwal during his days at SIBM Pune and together, they dreamt of making it big one day. The dream became a reality when through Yogesh's Pudhari Publications, they successfully bid for a radio licence in 2006 and started India's first Marathi-language FM radio station –94.3 Tomato FM– in Kolhapur and Sangli in Maharashtra. Their story is one of constant struggle against huge odds, of finding success in an arena where even the big guns have struggled and finally, finding their destination on this path of entrepreneurship.

Carrying the legacy of a publishing house with a history of over 100 years and especially that of a leading newspaper with a history of over 65 years is no child's play. However, winning came naturally to Yogesh. 'I took to the challenges like fish to water,' says Yogesh. At the young age of 17, he was amongst the top 10 shooters in India and had broken the national record in the air rifle category.

As a young man, Yogesh went on choosing the right kind of education for his eventual goal. He completed his Bachelor's degree in Commerce only to join the Bachelor's course in Communication and Journalism. As soon as he completed his Journalism degree, he joined the MBA programme, first at the Institute of Management Education (IME) run by Pune's management guru Dr P.C. Shejwalkar and then at SIBM. Even as a young student at these institutes, Yogesh had a keen eye for spotting talent, a sure sign of an entrepreneur. At SIBM, he spotted Naval Toshniwal, who eventually became the CEO of 94.3 Tomato FM, after a successful stint in marketing at Pudhari Publications.

'I met Yogesh at SIBM Pune and we really hit it off from the word go. We were a group of five and would indulge ourselves in anything but academia,' shares Naval.

'Naval and I were always on the lookout for some exciting opportunity,' adds Yogesh. Both Yogesh and Naval came from business families and given the right venture, were ready to take the plunge. As fate would have it, a venture did not materialize immediately after MBA. Both of them graduated in 2003; Naval went ahead and joined a company called IRIS in Mumbai while Yogesh assumed responsibilities at Pudhari Publications. Five months into the job, Naval realized that his job was not for him.

Yogesh was then plotting the success of Pudhari. Since they had never lost touch and also since he had complete faith in Naval's capabilities, Yogesh offered him an important position at Pudhari with the condition of relocating to Kolhapur. Naval willingly obliged since he anyway wanted to go to Kolhapur and help his family business grow. He started looking after the marketing activities of Pudhari with remarkable success. Pudhari was started by Yogesh's grandfather in 1939, way before India's independence and had grown to become the third largest Marathi newspaper in Maharashtra. It had a loyal readership in cities like Kolhapur, Sangli, Solapur and Satara and was rapidly expanding to larger urban centres. The business was perceived as old and orthodox and Yogesh wanted to rejuvenate Pudhari's image to carry the legacy forward into the twenty-first century. 'I had the ambition of developing Pudhari into a fully integrated media conglomerate,' confides Yogesh.

While at Pudhari, Naval also cut his teeth into entrepreneurship, first by helping his family business of power-cutting tools and then by independently taking up a franchisee for Amaron Batteries. But both could not retain his interest for long. In 2005, the Ministry of Information and Broadcasting (MIB) announced its policy for the second phase of privatization in the FM radio space and this was when the duo of Yogesh and Naval smelt their opportunity to create something together. The first phase of licensing in the year 2000 had not been a rousing success. Only the big cities were auctioned off and the interest had been limited to say the least. Many of the radio stations had lost money and were on the verge of shutting down. This time around, the policy was much friendlier and covered more than 300 channels in 90 cities. The opportunity had presented itself and our daring duo was eager with anticipation.

'When we read the policy document, we knew that we had found our calling. We decided to do our own research and went about meeting a lot of people in the industry. Radio had been a monopoly for such a long time that very few trained personnel or technical know-how existed outside of Prasar Bharti. It was difficult at first and we were constantly being approached by consultants but we persisted. Through contacts, we visited radio stations in Mumbai, Pune and Bangalore that were set up during phase one. We also talked to a few stations in the US and Europe to understand their business models. We even understood the technicalities of the operation through radio equipment vendors and that turned out to be a boon later on. It was all part of the learning curve and we were very thorough with our ground-work. Finally, we decided to bid for radio licences for Kolhapur and Sangli.'

The auction for phase two took place in January 2006 in Delhi. Yogesh and Naval were there along with many other stalwarts of the industry. These two young lads were up against much bigger and accomplished competitors but oddly enough, encouragement arrived from the most unexpected source. Officials at the MIB were quite helpful to these two young men wanting to be a part of India's rapid progress. They helped out with the paperwork and made sure that the process was conducted smoothly.

'It was a closed auction and we had made our bid for Kolhapur and Sangli. There were eight other players competing for the same two stations and only two licences were to be allotted in these cities. The tension was palpable as the bids were being opened. Kolhapur came up; the first licence was awarded to Radio Mirchi at quite a high price. Looking at that figure, we thought we were done for. We had bid a measly one-third of what Radio Mirchi had bid. But out of nowhere, like a ray of light peeping through the clouds, the under-secretary looked at us and signalled a thumbs-up. We won the second licence and that, too, at a much lower price. We were beyond joy; it was a feeling of sheer euphoria. We won the licence for Sangli as well at a modest bid. Our moment had come and we had won the first battle but the road ahead was long and treacherous.'

Having secured the licences, the next step was to set up the radio station and related paraphernalia. Most of the radio and transmitter equipment was to be imported and to aid in negotiating with the vendors, so the duo created a consortium of radio stations to drive a collective bargain. The location for the station was also carefully chosen so as to maintain easy connectivity with the radio tower at the Panhala fort in Kolhapur.

'Being in the media space, we knew how the revenue side of the business would work but the technical and operational set-up was something that we had to learn alongside. To establish a station-to-tower link, we pioneered the use of WiMAX technology aided as we were by Motorola. We bought our transmitter from Eddystone, a British company, which was out of favour in India but had been a technology leader earlier (it had the lowest power consumption). Slowly and steadily, the pieces were coming together and our keen sense of business was our only driving force. We drove hard bargains in all our negotiations, keeping our costs down to the minimum. We were able to complete our entire set-up at two-thirds of the budgeted CAPEX. Later on, we found out that this was about half the cost incurred by Radio Mirchi for its set-up in Kolhapur.'

Naval worked shoulder to shoulder with Yogesh through the launch of the radio station. While all the finances came from Yogesh and Pudhari Publications, Naval took up the challenge of building the radio station through sheer hard work coupled with creativity. While Yogesh was forced to juggle his time between strengthening Pudhari and launching the radio station, Naval was relieved of his responsibilities at Pudhari and was assigned the exclusive responsibility as the CEO of Tomato FM.

Yogesh and Naval, through sheer force of will, had accomplished the impossible. Their radio station was completed in a record time of eight months. The next step was in finding the right people to run the station and this was no mean feat. There were hardly any trained technical personnel in India outside of Prasar Bharti and even the creative talent was to be found mostly in the metros. Radio Mirchi hired from Mumbai or Pune and trained them under the existing staff but Pudhari had no such luxuries. Also, they were adamant in filling up all their positions locally.

'We believe that radio is a very personal medium when used correctly. A radio jockey can really speak to the audience and connect with listeners in a manner impossible through other forms of mass media. So our content strategy was to make the radio as "Kolhapuri" as possible. The jocks would always speak in the Kolhapuri dialect and we would play local music and focus on local issues as much as possible. To accomplish this, it was imperative that our employees knew and understood the Kolhapuri way of life. So, we hired locally and yes, it was difficult; nobody had worked at a radio station before. But, our vendors had agreed to train our staff. Moreover, talent in a country like India can be found in all places. We had a 55-year-old jockey and an 18-year-old girl as well. We wanted to cater to a wide audience during various times of the day. We did not want to be a lifeless clone of an FM channel in the metros. We were Kolhapurites and proud of it and thus was born Radio Tomato—*Ekdum Fresh.*'

Radio Tomato (94.3 FM) went live in late 2007 and since that day has captured the imagination of people of Kolhapur and surrounding areas. All jockeying is in the local language only and about 25 per cent of the songs are also in the local language. It even features local issues as part of its coverage and has had two OB vans in its arsenal since day one. Local correspondents have been identified in various areas. Many local administrators and celebrities have been featured on its programmes. When it comes to infotainment, the only name that rings in Kolhapur is Radio Tomato.

Though it was traditional in certain ways, it did not mean Radio Tomato was boring. It did have its MTV moments. One such event was a special con programme Radio Tomato conducted on 1 April. The most popular RJ of Radio Tomato fell prey to the prank and was left stranded with a red rose in his hands so as to be easily identified by a girl he was supposedly meeting. This entire con was aired live as the listeners were updated about the RJ and his most recent location. The programme became a phenomenon and hordes of Kolhapurites gathered at various 'chowks' to see the con live in action. This event not only popularized Radio Tomato in Kolhapur but also made the duo realize that what they had in their hands was a very powerful medium which could bridge gaps and bring people together. The duo kept this in mind and later used their channel to address a lot of public issues in the Kolhapur and Sangli districts, just the way Pudhari did.

Since the radio tower is at a considerable altitude, it is able to reach not just Kolhapur but Sangli, Solapur and parts of

Satara as well (a potential audience of eight million listeners). In listenership surveys carried out in the area, Radio Tomato consistently beat Radio Mirchi with a market share of about three times that of Radio Mirchi. Radio Mirchi might be the national number one but in Kolhapur, it is Radio Tomato that rules the airwaves. The wide reach of Radio Tomato allowed Yogesh and Naval to experiment with a completely different format and called it 'APLA FM 91.9 (Our FM)'. Thus, effectively, they have two radio stations in Sangli!

Coming from business families, their hunger is far from satiated and they are eagerly awaiting the third round of auctions to begin. Looking at their amazing success without any prior experience, we can only imagine what the duo would do with the experience they have amassed with Radio Tomato and APLA FM. When asked if they would be willing to replicate their model outside Maharashtra, pat comes the reply from Yogesh, 'No! We believe we don't understand any state better than we understand Maharashtra and as of now, we do not have the ego which would force us to be present everywhere. We would like to stick to what we do best and always maintain the image of a Marathi radio channel.'

On being probed about their future plans, their eyes light up and one cannot miss the child-like enthusiasm with which Naval confides, 'We have collaborated with the Marathi film industry on a different level altogether and in the near future, one would get to hear a great deal about us and our ventures in this industry.'

'All these years, we have been slowly building a network, a contact base and a name for ourselves in this industry and it would be only poetic justice that we make something noble and grand out of it,' adds Yogesh, who recently completed his doctoral studies in Media from the prestigious Mumbai University.

SUCCESS MANTRAS

'Believe in yourself, and never be daunted by competition.
Keep looking for new opportunities and ideas.
Always retain your enthusiasm.'

NAYAN ARVIND SHAH
Mayfair Housing Pvt. Ltd

Nayan Arvind Shah took risks and made bold decisions. Even after transforming Mayfair Housing Pvt. Ltd into a huge player in real estate, he isn't showing a single sign of slowing down.

∽

PERSEVERANCE PERSONIFIED

Nandhini Tamilselvan and Sandeep Suhag

The swanky office of Mayfair Housing Pvt. Ltd is quite impossible to miss even if it stands next to the impressive Mayfair Meridian. It is a sleek and modern structure and has a vibrant aura of energy. Moments after our arrival, Nayan Arvind Shah walks into the room, wearing a smartly tailored suit. At the age of 50, when most people aspire to slow down, the CEO of Mayfair Housing Pvt. Ltd is passionate about life and forever willing to push the envelope. From being the first Indian in the age group of 50-plus to complete the Ironman Triathlon in Mexico to pursuing his PhD, he has done it all. 'I want to attempt scaling the Mount Everest and complete another Full Ironman race within 12 hours,' he says, bubbling with energy like a small child.

During his days as a youngster, Nayan was fascinated by the armed forces. He considered them to be perfect people: well-dressed, well-behaved and of course, disciplined. As a youngster, he decided that he wanted to be an air force pilot. As he grew older, he developed an interest in other facets of life. However, he kept observing what he viewed as the perfect lifestyle: that of the armed personnel.

During his early school days, he was a mediocre student and just about scored enough to be able to clear his exams. However, when he was in the eighth standard, his father admitted him to Jamnabai Narsee Multipurpose Higher Secondary School. This shift was a blessing. 'The four years of learning in Jamnabai is reflected in me now. The peer group, the diverse school activities, proactive teachers and a vast library really sharpened me and made me imaginative, yet humble. All these played a very important role in grooming my personality and my inner core.'

His interest in studies grew as he moved from SSC to HSC and then to B.Com. It was during his graduation that he fell for English Literature. He was one among only 14 students of the 40,000 students enrolled in Mumbai University who opted for English Literature as part of their course. He explains, 'I realized that literature may not fetch very high marks. But it does make a difference in our lives. Hence, the moment I got an opportunity to study it, I consciously decided on it for my personal happiness and satisfaction.' He also took a keen interest in writing and was a prolific contributor to many college journals.

Nayan hails from a Gujarati family in which concepts such as *nafa-nuksaan* and *fayde ka sauda* were inculcated in the kids during their childhood. He tried his hand at several small initiatives, which made him understand the nuances of business. He joyfully recollects a part-time job of selling surgical needles that he undertook back in school. During his college days, in order to make some quick bucks, he opened a tape recorder repair shop. He was very active in co-curricular activities right from the school days, was the general secretary of his college planning forum and a member of the English Literature Society.

As part of the planning forum, he organized many visits for students to factories such as Coca-Cola and Parle Biscuits. He also helped organize many career counselling sessions and got a chance to interact with many enterprising people. It was at this time that he decided to do something on his own.

Some decisions are made by us and others are made for us. But both change the path our lives takes. Coming from a business family, it was assumed that he, too, would follow the same professional path.

His father, Arvind M. Shah, who started Mayfair Housing in 1964, wanted his two sons to join his real estate business. He wanted his elder son Viren to join as a civil engineer and him to be the on the management front. After completing his education in the US, his brother decided to return to India. However, his mother could sense that her elder son had experienced the world of his dreams and would find it difficult to settle for anything less. So, he was asked to stay in the US and focus on his future. Nayan was asked to join the family business.

From the early 1960s when Mayfair was started till the late 1980s, the real estate business was not particularly lucrative. Since the income wasn't great, Nayan and his parents used to stay in a BHK flat in Mumbai. Accepting the method of work employed by his father proved to be difficult in the initial stages of his career he says, 'Several times, I used to criticize my father's way of doing business. He had a very simple way of doing everything. Sometimes I hurt his sentiments by questioning him but my mother was the key balancing person. Working with dad made me humble.'

The turning point in his career was hastened by a terrible personal loss. 'The sudden demise of my father in 1993 forced me to step in as the CEO at 33. I was young and not ready for the role. I wanted to spend more time learning the business under the shadow of my father. But that wasn't destined to happen.' As a second-generation entrepreneur, he did face his share of problems. Contrary to beliefs, joining an existing business wasn't a walk in the park. That he had a superiority complex didn't simplify matters either. Today, he admits, 'MBA had made me an arrogant person. For instance, there were these contractors who used to work for us. They would come in the morning, and then start deciding what work they would carry out during the day. That is how they functioned. Since I thought I was above others, I took time to learn and unlearn by looking at their style of working so that we could share a win-win relationship. They improved because of this and work happened exactly according to what I had in mind.'

He also made a few wrong investment decisions. When commercial projects in real estate were experiencing a boom, he decided to diversify and burnt his fingers. However, that experience taught him a lot. There were also times when he had to give up the leads in the absence of any common ground between the stakeholders and his ideology.

Challenges—there have been many. 'My transferable development rights (TDR) deal with Godrej in Vikhroli was a challenging period. Another unforgettable experience is bidding for a 125-square-kilometre Special Economic Zone (SEZ) near Mumbai. I came out as the number two bidder. Those two years of the bidding process taught me a lot and gave me tremendous exposure.'

All through his journey, he has been focused on doing justice to the legacy his father had left behind. Today, he is an active participant in various national and international real estate seminars along with being an active member and office bearer at Maharashtra Chamber of Housing Industry (MCHI) as its Vice President. He shows a keen interest in areas such as financial instruments in real estate like Real Estate Investment

Trusts (REIT), Real Estate Mutual Funds (REMF), Real Estate Venture Capital Funds (REVCF), the role and extent of foreign direct investment (FDI) in real estate, the role of TDR and its implications in urban development and has been thinking of ways to make quality affordable housing a reality in India.

He has focused on developing lands under reservation and undertaken the work of redevelopment of old societies with a personal touch—a concept known as 'Mayfair Upgrade'.

Shah truly exudes perseverance. Cervical spondylosis and lumbar root compression never deterred him from pursuing his passion. He decided to start working in early 2005 for marathons and since then has successfully completed nine marathons in and around Mumbai.

In 2010, he decided to run the Ironman race and under the able guidance of Dr Mihir Patki, chalked out a special training programme. And in November 2011, he created history by completing the Ironman Triathlon event at Cozumel, Mexico. It is a 3.86-kilometre swim, a 180.25-kilometre bike race and a full marathon of 42.195-kilometre, in all 224-kilometre that have to be completed within individual cut-off timings, along with the total time limit of 17 hours. He always keeps challenging himself and believes that the key to achieve anything is perseverance, exercise and meditation.

The life of an entrepreneur does not end at the office like those of others in a job. His work, his family, employees and all other stakeholders become a part of his life. This makes it very important for him to create some personal time for his family. He believes that an entrepreneur should realize that his business is only a part of his life and not his entire existence.

'My advice to young budding entrepreneurs is—learn to

balance your professional life with your personal life, give quality time to your family, go for holidays, spend time with your young children, else you will lose your family and your business both.'

Life's experiences have enriched him a lot. Reflecting on his his experiences, he says, 'There are two types of errors you can commit: "Errors of judgment" and "Errors of leaving your core competency". The key is to do what you are best at, opportunities to grow will always come but stick to what you are best at and what you think you can do to make your consumers happy.'

He believes that 'Family is that one institution on which you can rely fully in your difficult times, it gives you solace and the strength that one needs.' He gets full support from his family, which includes his mother, wife, two sons and his brother's family. He never shies away from seeking their help, advice or guidance..

He tries to spend quality time with his family—he goes for holidays, tries to have dinner with them almost every day. He devotes time to meditation, fitness, his family, trade and his continuous interest in studies; even during his busy schedules, he is pursuing a PhD. He has undertaken various 30-day Vipassana courses. 'Vipassana has taught me to approach life and business on the principle of—do your best, results will follow sooner or later,' he says.

He believes that entrepreneurs in the development sector need to focus on fulfilling India's demand for affordable housing; this is his dream and he is working towards pursuing it. 'I want to make Mayfair one of the top five real estate developers of India and want to be the leader of innovation and make affordable housing in the Mumbai Metropolitan Region (MMR) become a reality. My dream is that every household in MMR should have a house of its own as per their affordability. "Quality Affordable Housing for all in MMR", is my ultimate goal.'

Speaking about his ultimate aim in life, Nayan says, 'I believe that knowledge and wealth created by me is to be shared with the society at large. Also, I feel that it is my responsibility as an entrepreneur to always have a mission such that it motivates all stakeholders to strive for the betterment of the people at large and my mission is "Quality Affordable Housing for All". I want to leave a tradition and legacy for Mayfair as an institution.'

SUCCESS MANTRAS

'Choose a business which you enjoy the most and at which you are best. If you enjoy your work, you will certainly succeed. You have to be best at what you do.

'One thing that all entrepreneurs should realize is that money is only the means and not the end. The end is the satisfaction derived out of the whole experience.' He realized very early in his life, that it is not money but the experience and the knowledge that he would gain throughout his journey as an entrepreneur that mattered.

'Don't chase money; empower yourself in such a way that money chases you. If you do your business and satisfy your customers, they will look up to you and your products. I feel this is the philosophy that businesses need to adopt in order to grow. Give to customers what they want; read their mind, try to relate to them. They should connect with you and visualize you for the product.'

MINOCHER PATEL
Ecole Solitaire

He is among India's leading motivational speakers and corporate trainers and a well-known success and image coach. He is also the founder of Ecole Solitaire, India's first residential finishing school and international corporate training consultancy.

៛

NEVER GIVE UP ON YOUR DREAMS

Ayush Popli, Prashaant Jain and Vijay Pareek

The first sight of Minocher Patel's office gives you an exact idea of what to expect from him. Everything is extremely organized and neatly placed. Minocher Patel is very well-known as the Founder Director of Ecole Solitaire-India's first finishing school. Besides, he is also a leading motivational speaker and corporate trainer, and a success and image coach.

When we went to meet him, his punctuality surprised us. After forming an idea of what we wanted to know, he took us through the story of his life with a smile playing hide-and-seek on his lips. We heard him in awe. He went on speaking. By the time he had shared the highlights of his eventful life, it was easy to understand how he had scaled the topmost peak in his profession.

The first and foremost message that Minocher Patel wants to convey to all youngsters is that if he, coming from a normal middle class family can get success, so can anyone else.

Despite never achieving distinction all throughout his schooling or graduation, he believes that excelling in exams is not everything that one needs to achieve success in real life. The only force that drove him was his goal of becoming

India's best motivational speaker, for which he honestly put in all the hard work.

So focused on his objective was he that, merely 13 years after he set out on his own, Minocher was presented with the 'KATHA UK—Global Excellence Award' at the House of Lords, London, UK on 14 April 2011, for emerging as one of the best and most powerful, entertaining motivational speakers India has produced in recent times. Apart from this prestigious award, he has won numerous awards in the last decade that recognize his wealth of talent as India's leading motivational speaker and corporate trainer.

Minocher was never a topper at school or in college. 'Overall development of our personality was always emphasized more at home,' he says. So not in the 10th, not in 12th, not during graduation nor during his MBA course did he ever get any distinction. He says he would give a lot of credit to his mother who always eased the pressure whenever he got lower marks than expected. His dad was a strict disciplinarian and was also a source of great inspiration. The point he emphasizes here is that one doesn't have to be brilliant in studies to become something. After his matriculation, Minocher was in Ness Wadia College, Pune, for five years during which time he completed his graduation with specialization in Business Administration.

At this point in time, he vividly remembers the part that played a very important role in his life; his experience as a member of the student organization—AIESEC (Association internationale des étudiants en sciences économiques et commerciales)—which provides a platform for youth leadership development. Incidentally, he was also a founder member of the student organization's Pune chapter and had been involved with it since his first year. During this time, he also used to address groups of students and conduct seminars. Talking about his association, he recollects, 'I got an opportunity to decide on my interest in training. It gave me enough practice to develop my training skills because, every time a new batch of students joined AIESEC, we seniors had a responsibility to train them in subjects such as fund raising, marketing and selling skills.' That is where he realized his true calling and his own potential for it.

He also got selected for a programme called 'Train the trainer' being organized in West Germany (as it was known at that time), for which he had received a scholarship. There were students from over 50 countries and he won the first prize for the best presentation. From there, he also went to Finland for a similar programme and again won the first prize.

It was in Germany that a trainer once told him that he had a very unique and captivating style of delivery. He said, 'I am a trainer myself but after 10 minutes of listening to you, you captured my interest. You already have a great ability at a very young age of 20. You have it in you to be a great speaker.' The trainers at the Germany and Finland programmes were good role models for him. But the person who really inspired him as a trainer was Dr George Judah, the then Director of SIBM.

When he was starting out, he took feedback very seriously, which he still does. He was told that he had a very friendly style as a speaker and, therefore, it was suggested that he should always wear formal attire so that his audience never took him for granted. This has worked very well for him.

He acknowledges the fact that he had been very lucky since he knew what he wanted to become at a very early stage in life. Given the fact that he had got the best of training at the same time, he could not have asked for more. A very high quality of training provided to him at the age of 20 worked wonders for him. This training and advice gained from world-class trainers gave him the required confidence to face and enthral any kind of audience. He now knew how to work his way around to handle different kinds of audiences and their psychologies, to handle aggressive guys, questions and other such factors which you absolutely must know as a speaker. So, on his way back from Germany and Finland, he was clear that one day he would be a professional speaker.

While going through this phase, he also realized that most of the speakers at the time were very theoretical and could hardly relate with the practical aspects of life. During his MBA programme, he observed that professors used to teach a lot of theories, which he and his batchmates could never understand how they would be useful in real work life. These incidents convinced him that his content of training should be as practical as possible and should stick close to real life, which his audience could relate to. At this point he also realized that speakers in India take themselves too seriously. To avoid this, he decided to always add some humour in his lectures that would also abide to the adult learning principles and keep his audiences more involved and engaged.

One more important step that he took was that he never listened to other speakers initially as he didn't want his style to be affected. Although a lot of people had suggested that he watch the US or the great Indian speakers at that time, he never did. He always wanted to go with his own unique style. He was convinced that it would work and if it didn't, he would then fine-tune his style.

He always believed that just like food, his content should be presented in a manner that would be appetizingly pleasing to the audience. At the same time, he focused on his content being easily digestible to the audience by using humour, by being relaxed and not talking down to the audience—this later on, became a philosophy of his teaching.

Minocher tells us that whenever he comes across something truly interesting, he immediately starts thinking about how it can be incorporated in his speech. As a speaker, he has to play the role of the producer, the director, the scriptwriter and the actor himself.

Recalling the influence of Dr Judah, he points out that a good director must necessarily be a good speaker because he not only motivates people but influences them in a far more life altering way. At this point, he makes an important assertion that a good speaker also needs to market and brand him/herself well in order to open doors to many opportunities.

During this time of planning, which had begun right from the third year of his graduation, he always used to listen to his professors and constantly made notes of meaningful points made by people and mistakes which he needed to avoid. At the same time, he never wanted to emulate any of the speakers. He always found out gaps which existed between the audience and the speaker by conversing with the attendees. While researching on this, he always collected feedback about speakers and their sessions which he attended. Even during his corporate days, he used to attend the training programmes or for that matter, even talk to people with similar perspectives. He never wavered from his direction towards the future—that he must become a great speaker.

His first public seminar was just after he completed his MBA, when AIESEC had invited him to give a lecture on group discussion/personal interview training at the Symbiosis campus. He fondly recollects being delighted at finding his name come up in newspapers as an advertisement for his seminar. He gave that lecture and his audiences were thrilled. He was convinced of the skills he possessed when he experienced the response. After that, during his corporate career, he gave many free seminars and lectures for honing his skill and one day, was invited to speak at the Narsee Monjee campus. He recalls vividly how after the lecture, a few students had come up backstage and questioned him seriously on why did he not leave his corporate job and become a full-time trainer. For his second seminar in the same college, there was an interesting incident wherein two students, who had bought their tickets in black by paying double the ticket price for his seminar, conveyed to him the money spent was totally worth it. That was the time he realized he had now started building some brand value and his service was sellable. One important thing he mentioned was 'it is one thing to like what you do and something completely different for the audience to like it too'. He was then convinced that he was getting closer to his goals. By receiving this feedback, his conviction only got reinforced.

While doing his MBA, he decided that he had to build some credibility in the corporate world before training executives so that no one doubted his capability or exposure. With that in mind, he went on to become the Brand Manager for Vadilal where he worked from 1991 to 1996. During his three and a half years with the ice-cream division and a year and a half year with the dairy division, he had the opportunity to be a part of a new brand launch called 'Dairy Rich' under which the company launched milk products such as cheese, butter, milk and ghee. After that, he moved to Dubai, where he handled country management responsibilities for Bahrain, Oman and Qatar for FSL Dubai; all at the very young age of 28. In early 1998, he came back to India to start his own business. In these seven years of working in the corporate world, he gained enough exposure to know how the top executive of a company thinks or how a normal sales person works. He had spent time in five-star hotels of different countries in the Arab world and had taken local ST buses to travel to far-off villages in rural India. All this was to bring in more experience and credibility to his work as he had planned at the start of his corporate career.

During his stay in Dubai, he also saw huge potential for the Indians as the education system was lacking in social etiquette, was very low on Emotional Quotient, dressing quotient and so on. He also saw that many people went to the finishing schools in Switzerland to attend courses. He identified this as an opportunity to merge his coaching and public speaking skills and decided to open a finishing school in India. He felt that he would use marketing concepts and his speaking skills to sell this idea. He believed that it is not only important to have a good idea, but also to have a marketing plan for the same. Minocher always believes that he is a marketer by head and a trainer by heart, owing this a lot to his MBA in Marketing, at SIBM Pune. He returned to India at the beginning of 1998 and set up Ecole Solitaire—India's first residential finishing school and international corporate training consultancy for which Ecole Solitaire found a place in the Limca Book of Records in 2004. He won the national achievement award and is seen as the pioneer of etiquette training in the country.

He established Ecole Solitaire in Pune, a city globally known as an education hub preferred for the quality of education and its weather. Before he finally decided to start his own venture in 1998, he took about a year off, studying how finishing schools function, travelled to Switzerland for the same, developed material, researching, prospecting for clients and convincing them how this would benefit them. It was a big risk, considering the fact that he was 28 years of age and had left a well-paying job in Dubai. He recollects a voice in him that said if he were to ever do it, now was the time and that if he did not take the plunge now, he probably would never be able to do it. He believes that a lot of us tend to procrastinate, by saying that we would do it in another two or three years or till we have an assured source of income. He had his first break when he conducted a one-day session for Larsen & Toubro (L&T).

Even though he did not come from a business background, he took up the risk and put all his energy into making it a big success. He was based out of Pune then, which meant he would have long 12–14 hour working days with erratic timings coupled with frequent travel between Pune and Mumbai. He was a one-man army and would micro-manage all the jobs, right from designing brochures to meeting clients. In the initial days of an enterprise, one may not be able to afford a staff. Since he was in the finishing school business, he had to project the image of quality education but had a shoestring budget. He had to manage with minimal resources, cut corners to save costs. At the same time, he could not compromise on the quality of work.

He had a clear set of goals for himself giving himself two to three years to settle down in his new career. If things worked out according to his plan, he would continue, else he had a plan B. His fall-back option comprised returning to his previous career as a marketer, as he knew he was a MBA from a reputed institution and had some very good work experience under his belt.

He strongly believes that every human being in his lifetime needs to commit to a few years of *'seva'* for humanity. He believes that through his line of work, he could motivate people, make them confident and help them achieve their full potential. When most people get older or get retired, they would want to do some service, but his thought was that in case his entrepreneurial plan did not work out, he would look at this phase as his contribution to mankind and instead of doing it at the end of his career, he would do it in the earlier stage. Patel was mentally prepared to earn less and entered his business with a sense of service to mankind. It was this thought and attitude that took the pressure off his shoulders to make money in the initial part of the business. Money was never the motivation for him which made it easier to leave Dubai and come to India. It was his conviction and purity of intention about using the talent that he had to benefit more people that made him start on his own.

It is his personal belief that his speaking skills are God's gift—with the right opportunities that came along the way and the right media exposure that helped him establish himself in his early days. Citing one such instance, he talks about a programme that he had done in the early days of his career as a speaker with the Maharashtra State Police. Initially, during the press conference the journalist from *Bombay Times* had planned to interview the state police chief but after hearing

Patel in the press conference, the journalist was so impressed with his clarity of thought and empathy for the police force that he changed his plan to interview the state police chief and decided to interview Minocher instead. The next day the interview appeared on the front page of *Bombay Times*. There was no strategy involved, just the fact that he spoke his heart out, which impressed people. An MBA taught him how to respond to the press but the purity in his intent rang true with everyone in the conference hall. He says that nature conspires to help those human beings who are truly talented, ready to work hard and most importantly, have good intentions.

Talking about his support system, he recounts that he had support from his parents and his best friend from college days, Anil Goel. Goel stood by Minocher when he first expressed his desire to become a motivational speaker and to launch a finishing school. He does not hesitate in admitting to the fact that he might not have ventured out on his own, if he had not got the financial back-up from Anil in his initial days, when he was a greenhorn.

His parents were supportive but worried about his decision, as one would expect—especially since he was in Dubai at the time in a very good job and was doing very well for himself. It still brings a smile to his face when he recounts how his mother had reacted when he showed her the cheque of his first earning as a speaker. Once he proved that this was a sustainable career choice, their doubts started to fade.

Minocher feels that as a novice entrepreneur, one might face moments of self-doubt. But one should not let these thoughts ever deter him/her and must move ahead, as charged up as ever with grit and determination.

His mantra for success is simple—*'Clarity of Thought and Purity of Intention'*. As an entrepreneur one should have a crystal-clear vision of what he/she wants to do and at the same time, he/she needs to be a good human being. The latter point stems from the fact that Minocher believes most people depend way too much on intellect and not on karmic connections wherein people with a strong character have good things happening to them. Most people get frustrated when results don't match with expectations. He says if you are a good human being, good things will happen to you.

He believes in the power of happiness. His contention is that people focus a lot on being successful but not on being happy. He believes that there is no point in being successful if one cannot enjoy life and be happy.

Taking the education system head on, he strongly feels that the education system today puts a lot of stress on being successful and not on being good human beings. He is of the view that we are not taught self-awareness in our schools. Rather, on the contrary, focus on the self or pride in oneself is looked down upon. This is in stark contrast to the skewed individualistic culture of the west. In this process, he believes we worry too much about others and ignore ourselves completely. Most people do not realize their calling because they fail to devote sufficient time to understand what they wish to achieve and what their goals are in life. He believes we all should have our own philosophy to live our lives by.

He believes in the saying of the Bhagavad Gita—'To spiritually elevate oneself, one should do at least one good thing in a day for another human being, without expecting anything in return'. The Bhagavad Gita teaches us about the way we should live our lives. Unfortunately, this is not taught in most B-Schools. Our education system is focused on making us global managers, but not good human beings. He believes that the Bhagavad Gita is a management book and should be taught in each and every B-School. The teachings of the Bhagavad Gita are some of the most basic things that each and every student should know. Also, our education system does not focus on etiquette and social quotient. He believes that this is one of the major missing links between what the B-Schools are offering and what the corporates want.

Another interesting fact that comes across is that he believes that it is necessary for one to have goals to begin with. Although having set goals increases one's chances of being successful, it is definitely not guaranteed. What is really important is never to lose an opportunity and be the best at whatever you do—*'There are no rules, you make your own rules in life'*.

Minocher Patel's role model is JRD Tata. He believes that JRD Tata was very down-to-earth, humble and an incredible personality. He has a lot of respect for the Tata group of companies. He believes in running his organization like the way Tata organizations are run saying that if most other organizations followed this our country would benefit a lot. He makes it a point to talk about the values JRD Tata lived by in his seminars and workshops.

Today, when he looks back at his decision to quit his job, there is not an iota of regret. Once he took the call to become a motivational speaker, he has not looked back ever since. Even now, he immensely enjoys his work. Whether he is speaking with audiences in the country or abroad, he never seems to get tired of it. To put it in his words, once on stage he is on autopilot mode and bubbling with energy, even after all these years.

He recollects an incident once, when he had made a commitment to speak with students at a coaching class but then had fallen sick the day before the scheduled programme. Despite the high temperature he was running, he turned up at the venue, barely able to make it to the stage, but once he was on stage, he seemed completely rejuvenated and conducted the complete session without any interruptions from morning to evening. By evening he was running a high temperature once again. A similar thing happened the following day too. It was only after a couple of days of rest that he could get back to work again. It was then that he realized that when he was training he had extra energy and good health—it was like somebody up there was sending him a message that this is what he was sent to earth for. This incident helped him to re-commit to his goal and dream of being a speaker.

An author as well, Minocher's latest book is titled *Ordinary to Extraordinary—Your Pathway to Success and Happiness*. He is also working on a motivational talk show and an etiquette show for television, which are at the scripting stage and hopefully, should be aired before the end of 2014.

He wishes to interview successful people on television so that people come to know of these great personalities. He thinks that the youth do not have role models. To some extent, this is also due to the fact that the media focuses only on film stars, cricketers and other celebrities. There are a lot of other people who have done great things in their lives, but are unknown to many. They are heroes—who have come from normal middle class families and have worked hard to become business tycoons, education luminaries or excelling in other fields. Minocher Patel has himself met more than hundred such people. He got inspired by the work that they have done and he wants everybody else to know about them. Dr S.B. Majumdar is one such person, who has achieved a lot in his life and still continues to do a stellar job in the field of education.

Minocher's advice to people, who aspire to become speakers, is to work under a good speaker. That way they would gain practical experience and learn the techno-commercial aspects of this line. This is what some of the great speakers did when they first thought about pursuing this career option. Deepak Chopra, a great public speaker, was an assistant to Maharishi Mahesh Yogi for 14 years. It is very important to find the right guru. Doing that helps one to channellize one's efforts and energies in the right direction.

His message is, firstly achieve success by keeping values in place and make decent money out of it. You don't have to become a multi-millionaire overnight—it will happen over a period of time. Secondly, right from the beginning, value your relationships, your friends and your parents. Finally, whatever you do in life, make sure you are happy, make others happy and enjoy the journey.

SUCCESS MANTRAS

'It takes time in any profession to do quality work and build up one's credibility. Hence, one needs to have a lot of patience and perseverance to establish oneself in this profession.'

ASHWIN DEO
Trinity Vintners Pvt. Ltd

Most Indians believe that drinking wine is a formal affair. Through his venture Trinity Vintners Pvt. Ltd– Turning Point Wines, Ashwin Deo wants to establish that it is a cool drink to hang out with.

∽

'RAISING A TOAST TO THE SPIRITED'

Dhruv Talwar and Vivek V.

Ashwin Deo comes across as someone who can never rest on his laurels; instead, his hunger, passion and breathtaking desire to succeed are clearly visible during our conversation. Ashwin is the founder and Managing Director of Trinity Vintners Pvt. Ltd. He has had a fascinating journey in a field where only a few dare to enter, and now, he is all set to prove why his vision of entrepreneurship encompasses a lot more than what he has already achieved.

Ashwin's childhood was a typically normal one. He completed his schooling from Bishop Cotton School, Nagpur, he pursued his graduation in Commerce. At that point, his only ambition was to help his doting mother run their gas agency by getting more involved in its operations. There was a time when he also felt that he could convert his passion for music into a career. However, he was not sure if this would have been a sustainable choice given that he knew nobody in the industry.

Like many other youngsters, he opted for an MBA and got admission in SIBM Pune. At that time, he believed in the merit of getting a stable corporate job. He remembers, 'I got a job with HCL, but my heart was in advertising. I eventually joined Everest Advertising Agency, where I was a part of the client servicing team. While I enjoyed working with them, I realized that my lack of understanding about what's happening on the streets was stopping me from understanding business in a holistic manner.'

After a year and a half at Everest Advertising, Ashwin joined the UB group in their sales set-up where he spent several years in different places: Punjab (during the peak of terrorism activities in that area), Haryana, Himachal Pradesh, Goa, Maharashtra and others. In between, he had also spent a year in Kolkata in the brand management team, understanding the dynamics of different customers. When he looks back at his enjoyable stint at UB, he strongly believes that going out on the field really helped him understand the practicalities of the alcohol business in India—right from the nuances of manufacturing, to the regulations and rules that governed various states as well as understanding the basics of customer relationship management.

After seven momentous years with the UB group, Ashwin decided to join another liquor major—Diageo, where, among other assignments, he was the first from the Indian subsidiary to be posted outside the country as Country Manager for Myanmar as part of the strategy development team for India and China. Thereafter, he was briefly with Foster's as VP Sales and Marketing where he was responsible for taking Foster's beyond Maharashtra before embarking on a nine-year-long successful journey with Moët Hennessy, as Managing Director for South Asia. This was followed by a two-year stint as the head of Tiger Beer's Asia-Pacific operations. He reflects on the value of his experience with different set-ups, 'Companies such as Moët Hennessy and Diageo spend a lot of time in training, conducting seminars and sending executives abroad for wholesome learning experiences. This certainly helped me in opening up my mind while honing my ability to innovate and create. For example, a trip to Mexico to see how tequila is manufactured made me understand the process better than any textbook ever managed to.'

It was somewhere during 2007 that Ashwin realized that the wine industry was growing at a frantic pace and there was a real opportunity to make a difference in the space. The opportunity, he believed, lay in the fact that nobody was communicating with the younger audience or the non-drinkers of wine. The communication had to be done in a simple manner, and not in jargon-ridden language that has always been associated with wine. Post the Tiger Beer assignment, he finally decided to embark on the journey that was really his passion. And that is how Ashwin's entrepreneurial journey began. He called it Trinity Vintners Pvt. Ltd—Turning Point Wines.

Despite being in the alcohol beverage industry for around 25 years, Ashwin was very clear that the beverage he wanted to get his own venture started with was wine. He wanted to be part of a space that was growing but hadn't been tapped very well. Also, having been the country head of Moët Hennessy, he was thoroughly aware of the consumer behaviour in this segment. Moreover, most of the assignments in his corporate life dealt with start-ups, be it creating awareness for accomplished international brands pan-India or establishing international companies' operations in India. As he put forth very astutely, 'I was keen to develop a market for new categories rather than increase market share for existing products.'

How did the name Turning Point come to mind? Ashwin

believes that while there have been two major turning points in his life in the form of his education at SIBM and his tenure at Myanmar, his decision to become an entrepreneur is perhaps the biggest turning point of his life. He has tasted many a success in the corporate world, seen and overcome many failures too—but after 25 years of earning fame and building a reputation solely on the basis of his work, it all boiled down to one question: 'Is this really what I want to do going forward?' During his days at Everest, he felt that there he was not in sync with the ground realities of the industry and had a lot to learn. Today, life has come a full circle in a way that he believes that India's youngsters have not been given the opportunity to educate themselves in wine the way they could have. To change this, Ashwin had to make a move around the 'Turning Point'.

Setting up the business was not the easiest of tasks: Turning Point needed a tremendous amount of publicity to invite consumer and investor interest. Close friends like Sunil Lulla, MD of Times Network, Rahul Akerkar, owner of Indigo Restaurants and T.J. Venketeshwaran, Ashwin's batchmate from SIBM, were of great help and he shared his thoughts with them. He also acknowledges the role that his family played in providing emotional stability during this critical phase. 'You are used to a particular way of life, and then suddenly you decide to lead a life that is completely different. No matter how confident you may be, the spectre of uncertainty will always loom over your head in the initial few months. So the people who actually deserve the credit for this smooth transition are my wife and son. It's been a rough time for them, and their support and understanding has been a great source of confidence-boosting.'

The Turning Point show is managed by a five-member

team, including three people to take care of the sales, one person to handle the stores and dispatch and Ashwin, who is the focal point, taking care of all the business activities. Ashwin has divided the business into production, logistics, financial management and marketing and branding of the wines. The production of the wines is outsourced to York Wines located in Nasik. A dedicated team in this winery takes care of the entire process of winemaking, which includes growing grapes, harvesting, crushing and pressing, fermentation and bottling. The outbound logistics of loading and transportation of wines across Pune and Mumbai is taken care of by Ashwin himself for the time being as the business is still in the nascent stage. As finances play a crucial role in the business, it has been outsourced to a chartered accountancy firm. The thought behind outsourcing was to enable Ashwin to concentrate on his core requirement of the business, that is, marketing and branding of Turning Point wines.

India is not a nation of wine drinkers, but Ashwin is convinced that things can change for the better. 'Wine is traditionally considered to be a top-down business where the image is set at the top and consumption is driven towards the bottom. Currently, the per capita consumption of wine in India is 0.16 th of a teaspoon—so clearly, there is a dearth of wine consumers. In a country where 50 per cent of the population is below the age of 26, imagine the kind of market lying in front of you if you can simply draw a connection between wine and the youth. Youngsters today are spending a hefty amount buying bottles of vodka and quality whiskey—so price certainly is not stopping them from buying wine. The fact is that the perception that wine is a drink meant for the "old" and "formal" seems to be embedded in their minds—and this is exactly what I am trying to change through Turning Point. Everyone is concentrating on pairing food and wine. The wine and food pairing concept had come from the west where it was a course-by-course meal. In the west, prawns are cooked in a manner which highlights the produce—but it is doused with gravy in Indian cuisines. In India, the consumption occasion is pre-meal. If Indians are to consume wine, the only way to make them drink it is to make them believe that it's a cool drink to hang out with. Turning Point wines, therefore, are pairing wine and mood, not wine and food!'

Ashwin has his own principles when it comes to official work. He acts tough on people who do not put enough effort in a task even if the outcome was out of their bounds. Sincerity towards work is essential and every effort has to be taken to achieve the results. As he says, 'What you build in your career is not the money that you make during the initial years but the reputation and relationships you build over the years. The one thing that works in India is humility and that's the most important factor towards your relationships in corporate life.'

'I was never inspired by anybody; I was inspired only by ideas which could come from anyone. For example, if someone is walking faster than me in the morning, that inspires me to increase my speed. As Dr Judah, the Director of the Institute during our days at SIBM, used to say—you should never get overawed by the ambience around you, instead deal with situations as they come. I try to follow the same mantra,' he says.

Today, Ashwin is very satisfied with his life as it involves the one thing he loves to do—partying. Since the entertainment industry is a platform through which he can canvas for his product, he spends three to four nights a week in the market visiting bars and nightspots in various cities, meeting prospective partners who can take his product to the next level.

Work aside, Ashwin is an avid musician and enjoys singing, playing the guitar and the tabla. He enjoys reading, and feels that books on Steve Jobs and others like *Blue Ocean Strategy* by W. Chan Kim and Renée Mauborgne have been very influential and instrumental in developing his thought process.

SUCCESS MANTRAS

'The best way to learn the business is to walk the streets and learn from your experiences. There can be no better teacher than first-hand experiences and that's the only way you can cater to their requirements.

'If you are optimistic, you will look for opportunities—they exist in plenty!'

PRAKASH ROHERA
The Redwood Edge

A leading motivational speaker and corporate trainer who has conducted sessions in over twenty-five nations, Prakash Rohera hasn't cancelled a single session in his entire career. Given his motivation, that fact will remain unchanged.

∽

VOICE THAT INSPIRES

Shawn Francis and Mohit Agarwal

He is young, dynamic and makes an instant impact with his positive thinking and attitude towards life. Not surprising, since Prakash Rohera is a motivational speaker and corporate trainer. He established his corporate training set-up, The Redwood Edge, in 1997 and has conducted more than 2,000 training sessions for over one hundred clients covering one hundred thousand participants in over twenty five countries—Australia, Bahrain, China, England, Singapore, Thailand, Turkey, the United States and the UAE, among others.

A poster which reads 'The spotlight is on you' is the first thing you will notice when you walk into The Redwood Edge, Prakash Rohera's office in upmarket Pune. The walls are decorated with fan mail and accolades he has received from heads of organizations all over the world. That is when one knows that here is a guy who has made it. Transcending geographies and cultures is an amazing feat for a corporate trainer. But Prakash has done it with ease. As is the case with many enterprising individuals who are willing to go with the dictates of their heart, corporate and motivating training didn't happen to him at the outset of his career. His career path was a conventional one, with his college education beginning by graduation in Chemistry from Hindu College in Delhi University followed by a management degree from SIBM Pune. He started out as a professional with HCL. Citibank and Bank of America taught him several important lessons till destiny and passion combined to take him on the path of training.

'I think the career path in those times was very limited. It was either medicine or engineering. Engineering wasn't my cup of tea, and it was nice and glamorous to say "I want to be a doctor." I tried the medicine route, but I didn't clear the entrance exam. Hence, that avenue was closed for me.'

After completion of his Bachelors in Science, Prakash grappled with his career choices and like many aspiring youngsters today, his thoughts turned to management courses.

He joined the Symbiosis Institute of Business Management (SIBM). 'It was a tough journey, a very chequered one, but life took a new turn, became more streamlined. SIBM taught me leadership, it gave me an identity'.

The going, however, was tough. Prakash's father was working with the Reserve Bank of India and his mother was a homemaker. 'Doing an MBA was definitely a strain on the resources for my parents. Hence, like any other middle class student, I had to make my share of compromises and there was a lot of pressure on me. I did part-time jobs while I was doing my MBA. I would to sell my voice to the Film and Television Institute of India, Pune and I would get something like ₹15 for an hour. But that was important for me because I needed that money.'

Talking about his professional career before he established The Redwood Edge, he says, 'HCL taught me how to sell, Citibank taught me how to train and Bank of America taught me how to run a business unit.' Now when he looks back at his career, everything falls into place like a neatly fitted jigsaw puzzle.

'HCL was my first job. It was a campus placement and I was very thrilled. My job was selling computers door to door. During that time, I got a job offer from Citibank. I went for the interview. I guess since my father was a banker, I always had this desire to work in a financial institution. HCL was fantastic for me. No doubt about it. But Citibank was the exposure I needed in terms of banking.'

Prakash joined the frontline at the branch. He says, 'The mistakes I made at HCL helped me bridge certain gaps when I joined Citibank. At HCL, I had to sell computers from day one. I struggled like crazy. That is why I don't believe it when people say "You were born a sales guy." It's a skill that has to be learned, and you learn with the inputs given to you, the experience and the involvement.'

While working with the Citibank where he was an Assistant Manager and a Branch Manager for around three years, corporate training happened to Prakash. He was doing a workshop for new hires, when the country head walked in. Prakash's intrinsic flair shone through and before he knew it, he was off to Manila to be trained as a trainer for Citibank. Finally, he was doing what he was most passionate about.

It was at this time that Bank of America entered the Indian arena. To set up their retail business, they need for a full-time HR professional trainer with prior retail experience. It was as if someone had tailored the job description especially for Prakash. Life then was wonderful. As a trainer in a multinational organization he was learning, travelling, making decent money and living the good life till the asthmatic attack in 1996.

'I didn't know what to do. Even if I went back to a job, there was always the worry of getting another attack. So it was a very uncertain period. I chose Pune, a city I had always loved, while doing my MBA. I bought a small apartment here and started life from scratch. I started calling up people and telling them that I was on my own and into training. It was tough to get my first client. My first workshop as an entrepreneur was at the Indira Institute of Management. It took me a while to set the ball rolling and the family was right behind me in this journey.'

The year proved to be a learning experience and a turning point in his career. Before coming down to Pune, he had been based in Delhi, which hadn't worked for him. 'I had had a spate of severe asthma attacks. My lungs were down to almost 21 per cent and I was in and out of hospital for 11 months. I couldn't even walk. It was crazy. Pollution in Delhi was probably the one reason. If that had not happened, would I have been an entrepreneur? I really don't know. But I had to face the realities of life which were staring at me—no job, two daughters aged three years and three months respectively. My wife was a homemaker. My father had retired. So I needed to get it going.'

Prakash's initial battles were tough. But that is when life taught him a lesson. 'That is when I learned the three Fs in life—flight, fright or fight. My family and I chose to fight.' It was during this difficult period that Prakash came up with the name The Redwood Edge that would be the name of his corporate training set-up.

'I had gone to attend a workshop in California, while I was the Assistant Vice President and Regional Customer Service and Operations Head with the Bank of America. Just after that I got an attack—I was on my hospital bed going through photographs and I saw this redwood forest in California. I remembered being told that they fight among themselves for oxygen. Whichever tree fights for oxygen grows taller. So tall are they that they are the tallest trees in the world and so broad that you can drive a car through its trunk. That became my inspiration—strength, stability and growth.'

One asks him about his wife and how he balances his professional and personal life.'Sangeeta has been like a rock. When I started on my own, I remember my wife telling me, "I didn't marry a Bank America, I married Prakash." Once I was doing a workshop for a client in Hyderabad and my daughter was in the ICU in Pune. I didn't know that. She explained, "If I had called you, the workshop would have got affected." It was a leadership workshop for the client. When I reached Pune, they took me straight to the ICU. So who is the star? My wife Sangeeta!'

Prakash pauses to take a sip of coffee. He admits, 'Yes, my work demands long hours and a lot of travelling but when I am back, I just have a ball. One option is quality time and the other is quantity time. One should focus on quality time. Yes, we have some rules. We take two vacations a year. So that is absolutely family time. Nothing else comes in between. We are a very close-knit family. We've got two daughters. So we are just four of us and my sister's family. My parents passed away so we all became pillars for each other.'

The one thing that comes across strongly when you speak with Prakash is that the guy exudes passion. That is one thing that he wants young, budding entrepreneurs to have.'I think the best thing for us to do in this one's life is to be able to see what your calling is and get the maximum out of it. That's my advice is to all people: find out what you love doing. I am so happy because today we have moved away from conventional careers to so many alternate careers. Whatever you do, you have to enjoy it.'

How does he define entrepreneurship? Prakash replies, 'It's being able to create a spirit of driving business with one's own resources and being resourceful without worrying too much and guiding one's self and team to a new adventure trail. To me, it is a mindset and a lifestyle and the process of enjoying building it brick by brick. If one is good and believes in oneself, business will come; if not right away, then, maybe, a little later.'

He says, 'In life, like I said earlier, there are three options—flight, fright or fight. The choice is yours. Choose to fight. Work on yourselves as individuals, as human beings, as professionals to become better than you were yesterday. I hope the concept of being honest with yourself and the people around you doesn't go out of fashion. Only then will people value you. One has to be true to one's self and be called credible and competent. The problem in life for many people is not that they didn't reach their dreams. The tragedy in life is that they didn't have any dreams. So have your dreams. Somewhere down the line, those words like vision, strategy and path will all make sense.'

Prakash has come a long way since the days he sold computers at HCL. There was an instance when a client told him that dogs and salesmen weren't allowed in his office. Even today after nearly 2000 sessions, Prakash is as nervous and charged up as he was when he started his training firm. He strongly believes each session is an opportunity to learn and train better.

The one thing that strikes one as fantastic is that Prakash

has never cancelled a single workshop ever. But there was this one time when he did come really close to doing so. 'Can you see that glass door through which you entered? About six years back, in 2008, I just slipped and fell through the door and slit my arm. Blood gushed forth like a fountain. This was on a Friday, but on Monday I was in a workshop with a cast, after undergoing a six-hour-long surgery on Saturday in Jehangir hospital.' He adds, 'There are some beliefs one must have. It can be tough. It can be lonely and it's a test. It's your passion that will get you through. Like we say, "It's your life and you are the star and the spotlight is on you."'

Prakash's business mainly involves catering to his clients' needs. So the eventual multiplication of training workshops on leadership, passion and motivation seemed inevitable.

One must bear in mind that expansion is limited because, as Prakash puts it, one cannot do more than 365 days of training a year. Among his other activities, two self-help books are in the pipeline, one of which will be out very soon. Once again, his clients encouraged him to do something that was always at the back of his mind. Hence, the titles are *One Life, One Chance* and *Selling with Passion*.

Being a speaker does take its toll. At times Prakash finds it hard to keep himself upbeat 24X7.'When you are travelling so much and spending so much time away from the family, there are times when you feel a little less charged up. Of course, we are all human and error-prone. It is not that we will not have our off days. But, what the hell? That's life, right?' One agrees. He shares an anecdote. 'My dear friend Sanjeev's father is 90 years old. He is a doctor and he goes to his clinic every day. Once I asked him, "Uncle, how do you do it?" And he said,

"When the patients call me Doctor Sahib, I feel alive."'

Prakash's motto is 'Walk Tall Throughout My Life.' He says, 'I can't change the world, I know it. But I can change my corner of the world, which is my work, my home. That is what I want to keep doing till I am alive. Train and motivate people, be a facilitator in realizing their potential and maybe help them achieve their goals and in the process just make a little difference. Because frankly, that is all that I know and can do.' It is a philosophy that we can try to emulate.

We unfolded different phases of Prakash's journey during our interaction. And every phase was an experience in itself. As we proceed towards wrapping up the discussion, Prakash shares his closing thoughts.

SUCCESS MANTRAS

'We often hear "Life is the most precious gift". Hence, what we owe to life as a return gift is "make it big" and not long. Quality of life must outshine the quantity of time lived.

'Moving out of the comfort zone is change; winning this battle is breakthrough; sustaining it becomes one's USP; and that then becomes transformation.

'For me it's the journey of exploring a new "me" everyday—as it should be for all of us!'

UMESH KATRE
Spice Islands Apparels Ltd

Umesh Katre heads Spice Islands Apparels Ltd, a major player in the garment industry. After spending more than thirty years in the industry and scaling the topmost peak of his career, he still hasn't forgotten the lessons he learnt as a child.

∽

ON THE SPICE TRAIL

Mohit Agarwal and Vijay Pareek

Humility in an achiever is a lesson for youngsters who aspire to be like him. Umesh Katre is one such thorough gentleman. Umesh, who established Spice Islands Apparels Ltd in 1988, has over 30 years of experience in various aspects of textile production, marketing and exports. He has been a Managing Director of the company since 1994 and was appointed Chairman since the financial year 2002–03. Such a long journey, indeed, for someone whose family background is rooted in the services.

'My grandfather retired in pre-independent times after a career in the judiciary and my father belonged to the 1952 batch of the Indian Police Service. So I am a first-generation entrepreneur as far as the family is concerned,' recalls Umesh. As a child, he learnt the value of humility from his father. 'In 1975, after being in service for 23 years, my father was posted as the head of the western region of the CBI. Both of us used to be at the BEST bus stop as he never called for his police car. He used to take a bus to office from Breach Candy in Mumbai. This left an impression on me.'

Why did he enrol for an MBA programme in SIBM (then under the Pune University)? About this decision, he explains, 'In those days, we really didn't have too many streams. If you had done your B.Com then you would have four streams. You could have opted for CA, CS or probably law, as MBA was then an emerging field which was just a decade old. I did not want to get into a technical field and really did not have the stomach for sitting down and doing chartered accountancy because the two months of articleship that I did after my second year was disastrous. So I thought, let's take a call on doing an MBA. I got in and joined. Hence, I didn't go with any particular perspective.'

The first go-ahead Umesh Katre received was from his father, who said, 'Two generations in the service of the government is good enough. So you should go into the private sector, try and be your own master because you have the opportunity to do so.'

One of the early lessons learnt at B-School was to be competitive. 'Very early in B-School life, you realize that students and colleagues admitted to the programme have come through a competitive selection process and will, therefore, continue to maintain a high level of competitiveness to excel. So you have a very competitive environment and you are forced to perform.'

The first go-ahead Umesh Katre received was from his father. 'He told me, "Two generations in the service of the government is good enough. So you should go into the private sector, try and be your own master because you have the opportunity to do so."'

Since campus placements were not a norm at SIBM back then, Umesh Katre went job-hunting after his MBA. 'I chanced upon an ad for a marketing position in the Mafatlal Group. Considering that it was the third largest group in the country after Birla and Tata, I knew there would be job security. There would be diversity as well because they were into textiles, chemicals, petro-chemicals etc. Fresh out of MBA, I got selected as a management trainee along with two others. We all started with a stipend of ₹1,500 a month. It was a good break and I joined there in August 1980,' he says with gratitude.

On the day of his joining, he reported to the Director in-charge of personnel where he was informed that the Mafatlal Group had three factions. There had been a split amongst the family members, which broke up the group in three parts, each headed by one of the three brothers. Arvind Mafatlal headed Mafatlal Industries, Yogendra Mafatlal headed a group of companies under the name Sungrace while Rasesh Mafatlal headed a group of companies under the name Stanrose. The process of reallocating human resources had just concluded. He remembers, 'Due to the turmoil in the group back then, there was no formal induction process for MBAs. We were also expected to introduce ourselves to department heads and senior managers over the next two weeks. I was assigned to the acting CEO of the clothing division and my first task was to chart out the paper trail of the process flow from inquiry to the sale and delivery of a garment order. This involved interacting with a lot of persons dealing with the process flow.'

'After six months, I was given the charge of sales for the entire Mumbai region. I learned the ropes walking the street from store to store selling Mafatlal shirts. Readymade clothing was new in India at that time, and it gave me a brilliant opportunity to learn. I got confirmed at the end of one year under Rasesh Mafatlal's Stanrose Mafatlal Group. After another three months, I got the charge of the entire western region along with the additional functions of planning and production. Now it became extremely difficult for me to move elsewhere because no one was willing to give someone with fifteen months' experience a job equivalent to that of area sales head. That's why it became difficult for me to move. I worked with the Mafatlal Group for nine years until 1988. Another reason for staying was that I got married in 1985 and within 15 days, my dad got posted to Delhi. We moved into a company accommodation in Mumbai. The first priority now was to secure a shelter of my own and all other thoughts were kept on the backburner. For my sake, my father took up membership of an upcoming housing society with the understanding that I would fund the project beyond a nominal value which he would contribute. I therefore took a loan of one lakh from my employers,' he narrates.

'So in 1981, I was looking after the sales of the western region. In 1984, I was in-charge of all-India sales. It was not merely sales. I was dealing with a product that was fashionable and perishable, so the job involved product development too. I was involved in fabric design, styling, range, sales and distribution. It gave me an insight into what sells and how a product sells in a particular region. Many a time, I stood behind the sales counter to understand customers. During that time, we also launched two new products and linings, educated the tailors about how to do different collars with different charts and so on. It was fun to do so many things. That was until 1986, after which I was moved to the exports division.'

'This was an area that was directly handled by the Chief Executive. Therefore, I was working with him and also with the senior Vice-President of the company because the focus was on exports. We exported majorly to Russia (the then communist bloc) and to Europe too. It was a different and diverse experience altogether.'

'The turning point in my career was in 1987 when there was

a strike in a factory in Nadiad, Gujarat. In the exports scenario, the commitment to your customers is something you have to fulfil. Otherwise you are out of the market. We therefore lifted all the material from there, trucked it to Mumbai, stored it in a warehouse and then went searching for a sub-contractor. This was handled by me, along with a small team, over the next year and all the export orders were done in factory set-up in Mumbai, Kandla and in Bangalore.'

This was when he spotted an opportunity. 'That's when I began to nurse my first thoughts of starting on my own. By then my new house was complete and I moved out of the company accommodation. I had a small kitty of savings and in 1988, I decided to quit. By that time, one had learned the tricks of the trade. The burning question was how to fund it?'

In 1988, I had come into contact with Sonal Garments from the garment exporters club, a deal for acquiring customers for them was worked out. Upon doing so, I was given a one-year contract with two lakh rupees as compensation. Now that the basic financials were taken care of, I could afford some risk.'

'A friend of mine had got an agency from Reliance for a product called Lab and was responsible for market development. I set up my office along with his in a 400-square-feet portion of a 4000-square-feet apartment in Mumbai which belonged to a friend who had moved to the United Kingdom. The idea behind sharing office space was purely to share costs and pool common facilities. My work involved writing to clients and communicating with them about my new set-up and soliciting business, in general.'

'The name Spice Islands germinated from the thought that India is known as the land of spices and Mumbai was known as the city of seven islands.' Soon the firm received its first major order. 'A chief buyer from one of my clients approached me with the offer of doing six styles of shirts from a lot I had sampled for him during my stint with Mafatlal Group. The styles I chose translated to an order of 33,000 shirts—an exciting beginning. Now I had to figure out the financing, sourcing and organization. I asked two of the sub-contractors with whom I had worked earlier to join me and also roped in an experienced hand from Mafatlal Group to join this new venture. Help with the sourcing of fabric came from my uncle, whose classmate was a major textile mill owner in Mumbai. My father helped expedite the process of receiving credit from Vijaya Bank. That was the only help I took while setting up Spice Islands.'

One of the biggest turning points in his venture came early in March 1989 when an English client came down to Mumbai and asked him to deliver a trial lot of 1,800 shirts of a difficult style that the Mafatlal Group had turned down. This was just the opportunity he needed and he seized it with both hands. He delivered the consignment on time and ensured that the quality was topnotch. Soon orders were being diverted to Spice Islands and over a period of time, the client began sourcing a large chunk of orders from Spice Islands. In two years, all-India requirements were through Spice Islands, relationship that has continued till date. Post this he established his first manufacturing unit in Bhandup in 1990. It was a small place with 35 machines that could do some specialized work only. He later went on to expand it to about 15,000 square feet with 200 plus machines which catered to 40 per cent of the production capacity and the balance was outsourced to dedicated sub-contractors.

Having seen the ups and downs of the garment industry

in the country, he says that the journey has not been an easy one. He recalls how difficult it was to get funding, a licence for the factory and find skilled labour. Talking of roadblocks along the way, he distinctly recalls the era post-liberalization, the early 1990s when he used to face a number of disruptions at the first factory he set up at Bhandup. Regarding one such incident, he remembers how the local political parties instigated a strike at his factory and that was when he decided to build a larger 30,000 square feet plant at Bangalore so that his production remained unhindered—a textbook B-school case. The similarity ends there, however. Negotiating with the union and its leader and meeting the deadlines of the clients while maintaining the high quality standards are things that one learns only in the real world. He admits unabashedly that this was the most difficult time for him. It even led him to questioning his decision to be in the business.

At this juncture, he makes the important observation that our labour laws are archaic and no government has made any attempt to reform the industrial laws of the state. In spite of taking into consideration worker welfare, untoward incidents keep occurring due to the presence of unions and often make the entrepreneur feel hapless.

As they say, a man is what he makes of himself as he learns along the path of life and he learns the most by the mistakes he makes.

It was in 1995 that he decided to go public with his company, a decision which he says was taken in haste and not very well planned. Upon the advice of a close friend, he decided to list Spice Islands on the Bombay Stock Exchange, an act that he describes as the flavour of the season. During those days, the basic authorized capital required was ₹3 crore. He felt that he really didn't have to run door to door from one bank to another for funds required for expansion. The decision was also borne out of the fact that India was witnessing a lot of foreign investment and the market pundits were all gung ho about the great Indian growth story with the soaring stock market. The launch was extremely successful with the issue subscribed twice over and the valuation of the company sky rocketing overnight.

Despite the initial euphoria, in hindsight he says that he failed to analyse then if he really should have gone ahead with this decision. He explains why the decision wasn't a great one, 'Going public, frankly, was not based on an ideal scenario vis-à-vis requirement of funds towards planning of expansion, diversification and so on. Funds raised were for increasing capacities but did lack vision then to plan for 20 years ahead. The issue in 1995 was oversubscribed a little over two times despite coming at a premium of ₹25 to the then face value of ₹10 share.' Where did he err then? He admits, 'One had never envisaged the regulatory requirements which then were fairly simple, but grew quite complex over the next two decades, resulting in making the cost of small equities, raised through public, a very expensive stand to hold.'

An entrepreneur must have his eyes and ears open at all times. He cannot allow an opportunity to pass by. In his case, he laments that he failed to capitalize on an opportunity post the listing of his company. He did not tap the growing middle class and lost a golden opportunity to enter the domestic market with a brand of his own, as he was doing on foreign shores. He feels it is difficult for someone to make a mark in the garment industry with his own brand due to the level of competition and the costs associated with branding. He is behind many successful international brands such as Double Two, Peter Werth, ALS, Falmers, Mustang, Lincron and others. He and his English associate have also purchased the licence to the American brand—DrunknMunky for the rest of the world.

After the acquisition of the UK brand DrunknMunky, he admits that the last year or so has been difficult for him especially with the Euro crisis. There already exists a team of designers, graphic designers at the London office who handle this brand. He plans to purchase a few more brands. From being a manufacturer and supplier for foreign brands, he has now moved into managing a brand and with it, its supply chain.

THE ENTREPRENEURIAL SPIRIT

Umesh Katre seems to have a flair for dabbling with a number of ideas and this adventurous spirit of his is clearly visible. He fondly recollects becoming an angel investor by investing in a technology start-up in the field of audio systems named Accusonic. Talking about Acusonic, he informs, 'Accusonic is much very alive and kicking. It's a privately held company and excels in the manufacture and supply of control panel systems—a business at which the company has done very well.' He also collaborated with an architect friend and tried his hand at the construction business wherein he along with three of his friends purchased a plot of land in Malad and constructed flats. He also has the experience of managing an international school along with a few friends albeit for a very short time.

He has also made smart acquisitions, namely of Bhupco Alloys which he acquired solely for the purpose of real estate assets of the company. It was easier than buying real estate as he could then avoid the cumbersome legal process of purchase, duties and payments. He also has interests in dyes through AVA Organics.

As advice to those running start-ups, he recommends careful analyses of fund requirements and a cautious approach to launching an Initial Public Offering (IPO), especially in the current scenario. He believes that one needs to have a serious gameplan before going public. One needs to know exactly where the funds will go and what are the kind of returns one will make since one is now answerable to shareholders. To shareholders, the only parameter of prime interest is share price appreciation and not necessarily the performance of the company. He strongly believes in not manipulating share prices. He suggests having an indicative blueprint for the next 20 years at one's hand when making big decisions such as these. If these are not given adequate attention, they could turn out to be a millstone around your neck. He points to the various regulatory compliances that any firm needs to take care of as an additional burden. Even now, if one wishes to delist, the rules are equally rigorous and time-consuming.

He reveals that he has had very little attrition in the last 30 years. He goes on to say that most of the employees are the ones who had joined him when he began way back in 1989. Not for once does he refer to them as his employees but rather as a family. That is where most companies today fail. The members of this family celebrate together and stay together with the company providing interest-free loans for personal needs.

He also admits to being smitten by the art bug and has been collecting art for quite some time now. Among his other interests is his fondness for weapons and shikar, although the latter is now completely prohibited. He believes that this sport requires great mental strength. He also enjoys a bit if gardening every now and then. At the ripe age of 54, he still has a youngster in him somewhere who adds fuel to his passion for cars.

He is also very active socially and has been leading a fight against the municipal authorities. The local administration insists on chopping down trees to widen roads and build an infrastructure for an upcoming football stadium for a prominent politician. Along with a group of activists, he believes that local heritage needs to be preserved and cannot be destroyed in the name of development. He is currently leading the cause with the case in Bombay High Court and also on social media.

He was also involved in the Save the Tigers of Sahyadri Campaign, where he actively took part in a motorcycle rally to spread awareness. He has also been trying to help cancer patients by providing those whose prognosis reveals them to be in the early stages with the correct treatment. His venture has also sponsored a ward at the Siddhivinayak Ganapati cancer hospital at Miraj, in memory of his late father.

These endeavours are indicative of a person with a deep social conscience to go with his rich experience in the garments industry. It is interesting to note that he has been a part of the entire gamut of services that one can provide in the industry, in effect, the entire value chain.

He does not shy away from admitting that when he started off, his wife had her apprehensions. But, knowing his responsibility, he took care of certain aspects such as a shelter and an initial consultancy which translated into a steady income flow. During his early years, his wife supported him and she, at a friends instance, took up the job of carrying out data entry which was outsourced by Citibank (which used to handle the majority of the chunk of public issues). The pay was 35 paise for every form filled and from being a two-person team, this operation grew to a strength of over 130 employees on the roll until a few years ago. This was another entrepreneur in the making. It would not be a stretch to say that the entrepreneurial spirit ran in the family.

Having his priorities straight is one value he truly believes in. He proudly says that he does not entertain business on the weekend, which he has devoted as family time.

His family and friends are his source of strength. He likes to take time out and give himself time to think by retreating to his farmhouse.

SUCCESS MANTRAS

'Be diligent: Always research well before any important meeting or any interview. Show that you have put in the extra bit of hard work and gone that extra mile.

'Never over-promise: Never make promises you cannot keep. Here he refers to the Indian garment industry and the lackadaisical attitude of the exporters. We need to learn to keep our word. He believes Indians around the globe are known to talk too much. We need to keep information as close to the customer/client as possible. Discuss your problem with them. His emphasis on timely delivery, schedules and quality are evident by the fact that there is a separate website for the clients to track their orders and this is a part of the company philosophy as well.

'Do not reply to communications instantly: We are a generation of instant mails, messaging and so on. He also talks about not acting in haste to reply to clients, customers, business partners or even friends since he has seen umpteen instances of a relationship being ruined by making a promise in haste and not being able to live up to it. In many cases, it also allows for a heated situation to cool down if one does not get into the mode of an instant reply. Allowing for a break or a short passage of time before replying helps one gather one's thoughts and think them through thoroughly.'

Respect other cultures: In his line of business where people come from diverse backgrounds and cultures, it is extremely important to learn to respect the sentiment of others. One needs to learn the mannerisms and customs of other cultures as well. He is of the strong opinion that with the world shrinking, management schools need to include social etiquette in the curriculum as well.

PRASHANT BHASKAR
plugHR

Prashant Bhaskar has created the concept of plugHR, which sets up and runs HR departments for organizations. It is a unique success story others can only try to emulate.

∽

RISK IS A PERCEPTION

Udit Jajal and Ankit Malhotra

Prashant Bhaskar has had an illustrious career. Initially, he worked with start-up telecom companies like Hutchinson and BPL US West. At Hutchinson, he did roles of direct sales and channel sales that laid the foundation of his understanding of consumers. At BPL, he continued with the role of channel sales, but his operational territory increased manifold.

Later in his career, he contributed towards dotcom ventures like JobsAhead.com, where, as an early member, he led the sales operations and increased the team to over 70 members. His experience at JobsAhead was the closest to running his own venture and actually paved the way for his profile of a full-fledged entrepreneur. In fact, it was at JobsAhead that he picked up skills such as flexibility, speed and decision-making.

He then led IT-People.com as Country Head before creating the concept of plugHR—plugHR sets up and runs Human Resources (HR) departments for organizations. By simply signing up to the services, the client gets a full-fledged HR department running within 15 days. The client also gets HR delivery tools in the subscription, making it a truly plug-and-play model. *The Economic Times* reported plugHR as the 'Big Out-of-the-Box Idea' in its 'hiFlyer' section in December 2007.

Despite his stature, he is an unassuming and down-to-earth gentleman. He met us at one of the small canteens amongst many in the Pune University campus. Here we ordered 'The Tea', the popular reason that brings people together at this canteen. For two hours thereafter, his story kept us hooked.

According to Prashant, entrepreneurship can be triggered off because of a variety of reasons—it could well be in your blood, it may be a decision influenced by your closest of friends, or it could be triggered during your graduation, but one who is meant to be an entrepreneur takes the plunge sooner or later.

His parents being in the armed forces, Prashant travelled a lot and had an upbringing that fostered entrepreneurship. He completed his education up to the eighth standard in a small town called Karera, a place 31 kilometres away from Jhansi. It being a small school run by a paramilitary force (the Indo-Tibetan Border Police), the teachers were almost always very few, picked from the forces and had their own ceiling when it came to core academics. The school countered this limitation by keeping an overdose of sports, field activities, outdoors and a lot of free time. 'This was a blessing in disguise for students as we were always excited about our school and loved the space we always had. Without high-sounding degrees, those humble teachers, mostly JCOs and NCOs, created a very strong entrepreneurial foundation in us,' says Prashant with pride. The school was 'ITBP Public School, Karera', which he insists he must mention.

As he passed out from the eighth standard, his parents were transferred to Kinnaur, the second least populous district of Himachal Pradesh. The freezing place is very close to the Indo-China border. 'You have to have an entrepreneurial spirit to quickly adapt to the sweeping change. Without cribbing, you have to get down to looking for new friends, new clothing, new sports, and ingenious new ways of playing cricket.' The school being in a forward area (very close to the border), there were only four students in his class and there were hardly any teachers available. So it was all about finding out how to get things done. This adaptation is something very similar to what an entrepreneur has to do! 'So I used to ask my cousins studying in bigger schools in places like Delhi, and try to solve problems, and would always visit the World Book Fair in Delhi, without a miss.'

Prashant further explained that the journey from Shimla to Kinnaur is 15 hours long but the terrain is uncertain. 'So you are an entrepreneur just travelling that journey of the unknown; with your ability to manage the unknown: entrepreneurship.' The ability to manage the unknown also reduces fear as well as the inherent perception of risk. Risk is just that—a perception; it is only in the head! For him the 'biggest risk is to retire before you have created anything in life'. Thus the spirit of exploration, which was inculcated in his upbringing, was entrepreneurial.

Entrepreneurship is all about spotting a problem and then solving it with a lot of passion, says Prashant. A job-seeker looks at his capabilities first and then goes for the job accordingly. However, an entrepreneur looks at the problem first, weighs the alternatives, and if he wishes to solve it, he looks for someone who can solve the problem for him.

Prashant was once asked at a school to explain the phenomenon of entrepreneurship to school children. This is the example he used: 'Let us imagine that there are two students of the seventh standard—one is a job-seeker and the other is entrepreneurial. I go to the student who is the job-seeker with a problem on calculus. The student looks at it, does not understand it and so he declines. I then go to the entrepreneurial student and show him the same problem. The student looks at the numbers and the symbols, does not understand it but realizes that the problem involves numbers so is mathematical in nature, and he decides to solve it. He then asks: "How much will you pay me for this?" He agrees on ₹100. The student then goes to the 12th standard, looks for the top five students of the class, shows them the problem and lets them bid for the remuneration for solving the problem. Whoever agrees to it at the lowest pay, is given the problem to solve.' Using this illustration, he establishes his philosophy, 'Entrepreneurship is all about problem-solving and creating win-win situations'.

Prashant simply states that entrepreneurs are people who live in a different universe, untouched by the nitty-gritties of daily life. 'I play tennis two hours every day and for me, it forms the most important activity of the day'. He claims Roger Federer is his favourite player. 'Entrepreneurs are guilt-free! They do what they want to do! They may easily sleep till 12 noon without any hesitation whatsoever.'

He explains that entrepreneurs conserve their energy for the activities which they prioritize at the top. 'This prioritization does not come easily for a working professional. B-Schools prepare people for slogging unnecessarily.'

As a kid, Prashant wanted to become a scientist. He graduated in Physics, did his MBA in Marketing from SIBM, and then went on to study Venture Capital Management and Finance at Indian School of Business (ISB) Hyderabad. He is now running the show of plugHR Asia's first subscription-based HR department.

'Trying out new things is a way of life. I also taught Physics while studying at Punjab University. I managed to complete over 30 courses in Physics in the three years that I was there,' he says, adding, 'I was toying with an internships portal, a parenting website, an online cycle store and a youth training centre when the plugHR idea was pressing hard. Actually, the internships portal also saw light of day but I folded it up in a few months since plugHR needed complete attention and energy.' The success of plugHR shows that his decision to take this concept forward was the right one.

During Prashant's graduation days, paging services were launched in Punjab by Hutchinson. Young MBA trainees would come from Hutchinson to the Punjab University campus for surveys. Smartly dressed as they were, Prashant was attracted to them and their profession. He interacted with them and even helped get the surveys filled. 'They used to give me a target for the number of survey forms and I used to exceed their expectations every time. I used to get the forms filled and submit them at the Hutchinson cafeteria. I also interacted a lot with the trainees and used to ask them about MBA. In the process I also met the GM of Hutchinson.'

'During the same time, I got an offer to go for an interview at the Indian Military Academy. To my surprise I also got an offer from Hutchinson and was asked to meet the Area Manager at Ludhiana. There they asked me about the expected salary. I knew that a second lieutenant in the military then got around ₹4000. So that is what I asked for. To my surprise, they offered me a pay check of ₹5000. That was the first day that I felt the lure of an MBA.'

'People's thoughts are limited by their horizon. If you think of it, before aircraft existed, the thought of one used to make people laugh. You need to think out of the box. As for me, I believed in the idea and clearly saw the market opportunity. Also I understand that in a structured research, people do not go beyond a certain point while responding.'

'I had confidence in the idea. A few industry people that I had spoken to were positive. Also, in a job everything is predefined. I started realizing on my own that I can run faster than I could in a job. Because of all these reasons, I realized that this was the right thing to do and the right time to do it and told myself to just go for it. There is no eureka moment. It is a long process. But then again, you need an escape velocity to leave the job trap. Turning jobless is one's biggest test of entrepreneurship. I would go so far as to say that the first day of joblessness is one's first day of entrepreneurship.

'PlugHR was a concept. The biggest challenge for me was to prove that this concept was a gem and to do that quickly. Being able to attract young and bright minds at the conceptual stage was another issue. Forming a strong team was one of the main things that were going on in my mind.'

Prashant explains the concept behind plugHR. He informs, 'The idea was to create a highly productized HR delivery that is standard and replicable across the client environment. To achieve that, we broke down the HR delivery into key components like 1. Planning 2. Knowhow 3. Execution 4. Technology.'

It has two facets which align with his personal interests and goals:

- Personal Happiness—Prashant likes challenges and what better than participating with ambitious entrepreneurs in

driving people's side of their businesses. To make an impact in their business and to create great workplaces where team members happily build their career is highly satisfying.
- Professional Happiness—It is problem-solving that excites him. He believes it is where the opportunities lie. 'Find me a path-breaking work in the field of HR here, there isn't much, the whole space is crying for a re-construct; it's an entrepreneur's paradise, with opportunities galore, and we have just begun.'

'Why plugHR? It's the simplicity of the proposition that makes it hot. It's just a market opportunity.'

'I'm passionate about whatever I do in life. But at times, people get offended due to the sheer intensity of one's passion. For example, I sometimes get too passionate about solving the problems of my clients. But a lot of times, when the client does not look at the problem in the same way, he may feel hurt or ignored. The crux is that if you make the other person feel that he is ignorant about his problem, he may simply get offended. This is one thing which everyone who runs his own business should keep in mind.'

'My parents are entrepreneurs in their own right, though they both served in the armed forces. They have always been supportive of entrepreneurship and are always looking forward to new ideas. My wife is a telecom professional and earns well. A working wife is an angel investor, a godsend. If with all of this support, you can't set up something, then there is something terribly wrong with you.' He also remembers the exact words of his dad when he discussed with him his intention of leaving the high-paid job and starting his venture. The encouraging words of his dad were—'If you can't take this risk now, then what was the point of our grooming you?' His wife assured him in another interesting way; she said, 'The worst that can happen is that you'd go back to being a highly paid CEO somewhere'.

'I was always into reading. Right from the seventh standard, I used to enjoy reading, attended the World Book Fair in Delhi regularly. If I have to identify two greatest influences, I'd say reading and travelling. When I was in the sixth standard and my brother was in the fourth, my parents undertook a two-month road trip on our scooter (Bajaj 150). All four of us travelled in the scorching summer through Jhansi, Gwalior, Agra, Bharatpur, Jaipur, Delhi and back. Each day was a complete school in itself.'

SUCCESS MANTRAS

'Concentrate on building an organization. Entrepreneurs commit the mistake of doing too much hands-on. Building the organization should be a two-step process:

- Prove the concept: Go into the depth of the idea yourself, prove the strength of the concept, stay hands-on and develop a winning business model.
- Scaling the organization: Building team capabilities, where the entrepreneur should himself build team capabilities and not be too involved in the operational tasks.

Problem-solving is the trick. Also, when you plan to launch your business, two factors are very important.

- Build a good business model
- De-risk your business as much as you can

Another important factor is that you must keep an eye on the markets. Whatever you start will evolve with the years and you are bound to find sweet spots during the entire journey. In other words, you have to be patient.'

MUKUND DEOGAONKAR
First Energy

Mukund Deogaonkar has made a significant difference to the society. His company manufactures Oorja, an energy-efficient, biomass pellet stove developed in partnership with the Indian Institute of Science.

∽

HELPING HAND

Amit Chand and Yogesh Agarwal

He loves work. Going against the prevalent entrepreneurial concept of being an early starter, he started off on his own only when he believed he should. Leaving the cosy confines of a job at a multinational, his endeavour is a rare one for two reasons: the space in which he began and the approach he took.

An oft-repeated adage in B-Schools is that if one yearns to become an entrepreneur, start early and plan accordingly. The key arguments that support this approach are that when we are young, we are more enthusiastic, less averse to taking risks and lastly, early failure gives time to recover and learn from what one has been through.

Mukund Deogaonkar defies this stereotype. Guy turns 45, quits his job and starts all over again. The guiding principle remains the same though: love what you do. Never go through the motions. From his words, it is clear that this passion has helped him overcome all the hardships of walking that extra mile in a trail less familiar and at an age that isn't necessarily conducive to risk.

Sitting outside his cabin at his workplace, watching him discuss operational issues, it becomes apparent that some people do attract interest in them through a lasting first impression. 'It's been delayed and isn't happening, I can't listen to that for long, I will go to the place, stay there until the work is done... that's it.'

Eased into a conversation, we make the customary beginning—background. 'I am from a very small village, which had about 200 households. As a child and today as a person I never set myself a target of reaching a place in future. So it is never like I wanted to be an entrepreneur or I want to own a billion-dollar company. I always do what I like and so I enjoy the process of doing it.' Talking in a calm and composed manner, he adds, 'A blend of both intuitive thinking and structural thinking is necessary to evolve a business model. It need not be in the form of an entrepreneur, it should be on the basis of passion. It is about what you like and whether you would be doing it or not. It could be in any form.'

His idea about a blend of intuitive and structural thinking echoes the left brain–right brain theory and reveals the depth of thought he has given his MBA. Following this is his suggestion for MBA programmes across the country. 'Let people be original and then let college add structure. It's about assimilating data at the back of your mind and this is only possible if you are able to pick out those threads which are apt for a situation. The dots are your own. Nobody can teach you how to connect the dots because each person has his or her own experience. When we talk about connecting the dots, we mean the part of that experience we will pick up now and use in future. This cannot be taught.' It is a point well taken.

If MBA is all about thought, the application lies in what follows. True to his way of approaching things, First Energy is the result of a well-structured thought process whose seeds were sown in 2004. 'This journey (First Energy) started in 2004 with British Petroleum (BP). C.K. Prahalad was our mentor. We started because BP was the second largest oil company in the world but was not present in a large format in the second-most populous country in the world. So what is it that we could create—'(i) a business (ii) in the field of energy and (iii) scalable by BP standards. This was the line we started with.'

'While working with BP we thought that the rural market provided an excellent opportunity in energy. So this was a segment where we could scale up very fast. Our biggest pivot was to create systems that are sustainable for those geographies.' Growing up in such an environment as a youngster had given him an excellent understanding of what works in the rural market and how. It is through a combination of understanding and backing radically new technology that he arrived at a key product of his firm—Oorja, which means energy in Hindi, developed in partnership with the Indian Institute of Science. It is an energy-efficient, biomass pellet stove that can be used in households and restaurants in India. The website claims 50 per cent savings on fuel bills but the key saving is for rural households and is in the form of time.

He narrates an emotional real-life experience to illustrate the impact of the product. 'Once, we went to a village where there was a woman in a small two-room house. She had three children and was the bread-winner for the family. Her daily wages were around ₹130–140. I was stunned to see that she was using Oorja. A lady who was earning so little was spending on my product. For her, feeding five mouths wouldn't have been easy. I was touched. Her response to a query on the real benefits it gave her was an eye-opener. She told me that it saved a lot of time (close to two hours) which she could now use to earn more. That was when I felt that we were touching so many lives. That is when the realization dawned that this business should never be closed.'

He analyses the significance of the story. 'When you run a business, you have to be aware of things that are working and things that aren't. We had our own evolution in the business starting from villagers, rural households and on to a commercial stove where the value to the consumer is the highest. Had we been dogged and inflexible about the area we wanted to focus on, it wouldn't have worked. At BP, the objectives were different compared to ours when we started on our own. We didn't have deep pockets. So we had to find out ways to make it work at the least possible cost with the highest possible return. It took us almost a year to figure out what we can do to start making money. We were not making money in the home-use market and were bleeding a lot initially. That's when we started developing the product for commercial usage. This chunk of business is growing well today, but we have also let the original thought remain, which is the home-use segment.'

Right from the initial years, there have been two challenges that exist the way they did even today. People—the major challenge for an organization is people. It can't hire the talent it wants. It's like a one-man (or two in this case) army. One person has to do sales, operations, promotion, financing, expansion et al. As he says, 'I still can't hire the kind of talent I require in the organization, but I am sure we'll be able to do that very quickly. Our solution lies in the process of hiring talent for all departments of the organization till the time we get the right talent.' The second is that of money. You never have enough money to run a business. That's a problem because at every stage there is something more to do. He explains, 'One of the biggest things I keep telling people is that when you run a business, you can never think money. Your requirements keep going up, something more…something more…then you start hiring. After two years, you think you will have money. It doesn't happen that way.'

'You need to find out ways to manage money. The important thing businesses teach is the *worth of every penny spent*. If I were to look back at my corporate life, the biggest thing I have learnt is that large organizations spend a lot of time on smaller issues. Everyone is keen on protecting their own turf and in doing so waste a lot of resources and money. The worth of every resource is very high for us.'

This reflects the importance of the return on resource for businesses, often overlooked when working for someone else. Elaborating on the contrast between an entrepreneur and an employee, he says that entrepreneurship teaches humility. Unlike a corporate environment where one is aided and shielded by many others and knowledge reinforces knowledge, one is left to one's devices in an entrepreneurial set-up. It inevitably boils down to this—'If you know, you will deliver. Otherwise, you won't.'

'As a small firm, not many people entertain you. So it becomes difficult to engage people. When you are on your own, people just don't walk in as against the case when you were in BP or Castrol or for that matter, any MNC. So you get to rely a lot on personal skills. There comes a stage in the organization when you leverage your personal equity. By equity, I don't mean money but relationships, network and people. At some stage, you start leveraging organization equity but that is generally a long haul for any organization.'

It is time to learn more about the support structure. He tells us about the amazing support he has received from his wife and daughter. 'They were very kind in terms of letting me do what I wanted to do. The basic question involves what it takes to run your day-to-day life. If you can structure that and know that you can survive without money or salary for a certain time period, you can afford to do what you want if you are passionate enough.'

It is said that networking is the prop for any business. However, does it have similar importance in the energy business? 'Networking has helped me to have very good friends, people who really want to be friends. Fortunately, I have a lot of such friends. It's not about Facebook friends. I think those relationships matter. Other networks like Castrol and BP also help. The SIBM network has also come in handy.'

A partner in business is essentially a key ally, a person on whom we can rely on with full confidence. Mukund's partner Mahesh shares this mutual feeling. 'Both of us felt the same way. We are both accidental entrepreneurs. We have been doing what we wanted to do but in different ways. He (Mahesh) is a very talented person and we have been working together for a long time.'

Entrepreneurs are marathon runners and to last the distance, one needs passion, structured thought, support from family and friends and the right backing. Without a central guiding principle though, the flame would eventually die out in the face of obstacles. Mukund has derived a lot from the writings of Ayn Rand.

'Ayn Rand influenced me a lot. I read Ayn Rand in my first year. I think both her books (*The Fountainhead* and *Atlas Shrugged*) leave a lasting impression. They are like my bibles. I believe a lot in the theory she has. Believing in yourself and individuals around you is as significant as the structure around us. I have been carrying this philosophy all my life.'

The other person he seeks inspiration from is the late C.K. Prahalad. 'I admired him a lot. Not when I was pursuing my MBA but when we interacted at BP. He is like a father figure.' He admires N.R. Narayan Murthy for his values. 'His was the first time someone spoke about basing the fundamentals of an organization on integrity. He was not content with merely creating a business. He wanted to create a professional corporate body with the right underpinning.' Mukund reflects, 'Our whole endeavour is to follow some of those rudiments. We will not do something just for the sake of doing business. That's clear. We will follow values as business is the outcome of activities we do. The overall vision that we would never compromise on is ethics, integrity and honesty. We would not do anything for the sake of it. Business is not about an individual task. It's about people. That's more important than anything else. If we create value and people rather than only numbers, I'll be happy. The way I look at it is that I can't work where I can't enjoy. Our endeavour has been that this is the best we would like to give people.'

How does he unwind? 'I run a lot and I am a big fan of music. I strum. I can keep people engaged for a long time. I love running because it's like meditation for me. I derive a lot of peace from it.'

SUCCESS MANTRAS

'Entrepreneurs are marathon runners and to last the distance, one needs passion, structured thought, support from family and friends and the right backing. Without a central guiding principle though, the flame would eventually die out in the face of obstacles. It's like this—what is long-distance running? At some stage your body gives up. What sustains you is your mind. After running 16 kilometres, you won't be happy to run anymore. The only way you can push yourself further is through your mind.'

FALGUNI THAKKAR
ENABLE

Falguni Thakkar quit a secure corporate job to follow her dream. She now heads Enable, an organization that works with SMEs and corporates by partnering with them.

∽

ABLE TO ENABLE

Sofia Parveen and Surya Vardhan Azad

For women aspiring to be entrepreneurs, Falguni Thakkar's is an inspiring story, A Psychology graduate from St Xavier's College, Mumbai, Falguni went on to work with Wipro after getting placed on campus. After a successful stint at Wipro, she went down the path of entrepreneurship by starting her own Human Resource (HR) consulting firm to service Small and Medium Enterprises (SMEs).

What makes her story very inspiring is the fact that she left a cushy corporate job by taking the leap into the entrepreneurial realm in a field which had always been close to her heart—Human Resources. She now heads her venture Enable, and works closely with SMEs and corporates by partnering with them. Their raving reviews of Enable and Falguni are testimony to the fact that hers is an organization that is respected and looks set to attain heights in the time to come.

Falguni hails from a joint family in Gujarat's traditional Kutchi community. However, her upbringing was anything but traditional. As she says, 'My mother Bharati is an Economics graduate from Sophia College and a very forward-looking person. My father Jaysinh Thakkar is an engineer and has been always very conscious about helping those in need. My parents have raised me and my sister to be very independent people and always trusted us to do the right thing.'

Her uncle, who was the guardian of the household, favoured equality in terms of how boys and girls were to be brought up. 'I was extremely fortunate to be brought up in that family. My uncle laid a lot of stress on education for both boys and girls in the family, and anything less than a Master's degree was considered inadequate, a thought which was progressive for that time. The girls in the family were not pushed into getting married before their time, unlike the tradition at that time in the community. Had my uncle been alive today, he would have wanted me to do a PhD.'

The confidence that flashes across Falguni's face as she speaks has deeper roots. As a child, she was always encouraged to study, talk about things and give her view on almost any topic. 'Whenever there was a decision to be made in the household—even if a car was being bought—it was the children in the house who were made to take decisions, and adults did not involve themselves. So you were used to thinking things out, and contributing from a very young age. We were encouraged to vote for things and voice our opinion, and most importantly, encouraged to support our argument with sound logic.'

She wasn't exactly a very ambitious kid, and would largely go with the flow. 'It wasn't like I was sure of one thing, say, to become a pilot or a big-shot entrepreneur. It was a good, happy life with nothing to worry about.' However, those strong family roots in education gave her a desire to build and develop her intellectual self. After school she went to St Xavier's College, Mumbai University, and earned a BA (Honours) degree in Psychology.

'I had heard a lot about the kind of platform St Xavier's

provided its students and I was clear that I would study only there. I was intrigued by the concepts of social dynamics and individuals' behaviour in groups. It certainly helped that St Xavier's had a very good Psychology department with a great faculty. I undoubtedly had a great time there and learnt many things. It was the right choice as I loved my professors and excelled at what I was doing—I was a Merit Lister in SYJC'.

Her studies in Psychology had a major part to play in orienting herself to the field of HR. While in college she did a stint with a local NGO, AYBI—Association of Youth for a Better India—set up by budding entrepreneurs.

The NGO focused heavily on HR practices, such as plenary and visioning workshops, training workshops, team member engagement and running projects professionally, among other things. Falguni, after a while, went on to become a core committee member where she got an even closer view of Human Resource Management. 'I picked up a flair for HR policies and practices. I began to like the subject, and started appreciating its importance.'

This was the time when she decided to go for an MBA in HR, instead of going further in the development sector. 'There were two choices for me; one was social work and the other was to develop my HR skills. I was very clear I didn't want to be in Delhi, which is where all professional social work happened, while it wasn't the case in Mumbai. That's when I started warming up to the idea of an MBA. I thought I could always get into social work later if I ever wanted to. I was very clear that HR was the thing for me'.

She decided to have a back-up plan and enrolled herself in a Master's programme in Psychology at the Mumbai University as it allowed her to pursue a course in Organizational Psychology. This didn't turn out to be what she had hoped for. 'Two to three months down the line, I remember thinking that that wasn't for me because I thought I was degenerating in terms of education and in terms of what I had learned at St Xavier's. So I was very clear that MBA was the only option.'

She later appeared for the SNAP test in 1997 and cleared the cut-offs, earning a call from SIBM Pune, which she converted. While she does appreciate the role an MBA played in shaping her career, she doesn't go as far as to say that it prepares you to tread your own path, and is not sure if it has sown the entrepreneurial seed in her mind. 'I was reading an article written by a successful businessman in the UK in the current *Readers' Digest* edition. He says that all successful entrepreneurs are college drop-outs, including the likes of Steve Jobs, Bill Gates and Sir Richard Branson. His point is that all children are very good at marketing and at negotiating, and you can see that in their interactions with their parents—the way they are almost always able to get their way. It is the "graduation process" that makes you lose some of that ability. I believe that there is some merit to what he was saying as sometimes as an MBA your focus becomes too narrow, and at times it gives you a false ego. An entrepreneur cannot afford to do that and needs to keep in mind what is needed to be successful.'

She also acknowledges the fact that a lot of B-schools today realize that they need to play a role in motivating students to be entrepreneurs, and have courses and facilities for the same, such as entrepreneurial labs, mentorship and venture funding. She admits that this is something that wasn't provided to her but is the right way to go about.'

'Many B-schools today encourage the development of skills to become an entrepreneur because there are these different skills you need to have. It wasn't so geared towards entrepreneurship at our time as it is now. So, in my case, I think the seeds of entrepreneurship were sown much later in my career, but SIBM Pune did provide a base for me to become a good professional, which also proved important in the Enable journey.'

After going through the rigorous course at SIBM Pune, Falguni got placed on the very first day of the placement season in 1999 at Wipro Technologies. 'I am very fortunate that my mother and father were very supportive and enabled me to take all the opportunities that came my way, including joining Wipro at Bangalore. Many of my friends did not get such an open atmosphere to grow.'

'I was very lucky to get an opportunity to work at Wipro. I think it's a brilliant place to work especially from an HR perspective. I haven't seen many organizations that empower the HR professionals to the extent they do, and there are very few such organizations in India.'

She enjoyed a very successful stint at Wipro, and cites that as a reason for much of what she is today, calling herself a 'Wipro baby'. 'It was a great experience. I was just a fresher without much training and I was being made to deal with business unit heads. You were seen as a partner, and they treated you with a lot of respect and everyone listened to what you had to say. That kind of empowerment gives you a lot of space to learn, and so does the exposure to great HR practices at Wipro. Azim Premji admired Jack Welch a lot, and we were partners with GE, so we inculcated a lot of great HR practices from them.'

She started with group HR but was soon put into a line role. Line as in day-to-day HR at Wipro comprised life cycle activities, including induction, confirmation, performance management, training, talent and growth management and exits. Wipro being the strong HR-driven organization that it was, the line function exposed her to certain aspects of business that make a person understand business as a whole. While handling talent engagement in her second year at Wipro, she got to work on an assignment with the Cisco business unit, which brought with it a whole new set of challenges.

The Chinese company, Huawei, was giving Cisco stiff competition. 'Attrition became a very big issue at Cisco—more of a business issue than an HR one—so we used to have calls with the Cisco management team. Containing attrition was a job with a lot of responsibility, which made me learn a lot. I learnt how business and HR go hand in hand.'

She stayed at Wipro for seven years, and won many accolades during that time, while climbing up the hierarchical ladder at the same time.

She is credited with starting a whole new initiative at Wipro called MOJ—Moments of Joy, a fun initiative for employee engagement, the types of which are common now, but were ahead of its time then. 'It turned out to be something big for Wipro! It was something radical for the time. It was the sort of time when people who had dressed well to work were asked if it were their birthday. When it was launched, Wipro had no fun initiatives and this gave a platform for employees to mingle, have some fun and bust stress at the workplace,' she says.

She was later transitioned from Wipro Technologies to Wipro BPO. It was a company, Spectramind, that Wipro had acquired and the work culture differed greatly.

'I remember being told by Wipro Technologies' HR Head when I was leaving for Wipro BPO that I should not be saying things to the effect of, "Hey, this is not how it was at Wipro; this is what we used to do." But I did exactly that. It was a lesson I learnt never to repeat. Once I realized this and started understanding the business reality, I was able to be a part of the change initiative. The BPO stint also contributed much to my learning.'

In the early 2000s, when some of the top and middle management at Wipro started leaving to join Ashok Soota at MindTree, there was a lot of churn in the workforce at Wipro. She explains the reason behind the exodus, 'This was more employees of one division who left Wipro to join Mind Tree, the organization co-founded by Ashok Soota. I think that Soota was a very charismatic leader and also very technology-focused. That was a key reason.' The new management that came in was very optimistic about the future and set a vision of making it a $4 billion company by 2004. Falguni was selected to be in the taskforce set up to make that vision a reality.

'It was a great honour to have been chosen in that taskforce. We were nowhere close to achieving that at the time, but I got to see how a vision can be evolved and is rolled out. We became the world's first company to get the People Capability Maturity Model (PCMM) certificate in that timeframe.'

The big leap into entrepreneurship didn't happen until she actually left Wipro to take a break. 'While I had been learning a lot about managing Human Resources, the decision to start something on my own hadn't been building in my mind at all while I was at a Wipro. I had taken a break in 2006 after getting married because I thought I was getting burnt. Working at a BPO is tough work involving long hours; there were times when I did 20 hours at a stretch. So I decided to take a bit of a break, and thought that this was the perfect time to pursue my interests for some time.'

Two to three months into the break though, she being the hard-working professional that she is, got the itch to get back into office and start working again. 'I had started getting bored, and I decided that I had had enough of staying out of professional life.'

That's when she had a conversation with her father-in-law that changed her career path. Her father-in-law, a very successful entrepreneur himself, is the Managing Director of Premcem Gums Pvt. Ltd, a company that produces and sells guar gum to a wide variety of industries such as food, pet food and oil exploration. 'He advised me to start something on my own, and said that it was the perfect time to do that then.'

But she wasn't so sure. 'I remember thinking that I wasn't ready and not sure whether I had the capability of running a business.'

But her father-in-law was reassuring. 'He told me that I had worked for close to eight years, and successfully at that. He kept telling me that I could do it, and if it didn't work out, I could always go and get a job. Being the businessman that he is, he kept selling the idea to me until it was sold!'

That's when she realized that there were a lot of non-HR professionals who had set up businesses to provide non-recruitment HR solutions to companies, especially to SMEs. One even approached her, asking her to be the CEO of that organization. 'That's when I thought that instead of working for somebody else, I could set up that kind of business for myself, knowing I had the capability to do it.'

She already had some of the resources at her disposal. Her husband, who also worked at the family firm Premcem Gums, had space in his office she could use. 'I was very lucky that I had the infrastructure, because for many that becomes a roadblock.'

She set up Enable, an HR consultancy firm to service the requirements of companies in the SME sector and provide consulting services to larger companies, in October 2007.

'I chose to service the SMEs as I thought that was one of the sectors I could benefit the most. The larger companies have their own HR set-ups, and SME is the sector which is most growth-oriented in India and has the maximum potential.'

However, this had its own set of challenges which Falguni learnt along the journey. 'They have great challenges in attracting people, because there are these brand names. You ask young college graduates to work with an SME, and they shudder, much rather wanting to work with MNCs. The pay package in SMEs differs, and the work environment differs. If you are doing HR for an SME, you have a big challenge at hand. The SME also can't afford to pay you for consultation as much as a big company can. So it's a big battle—you're doing more work than you would for a big company and getting paid less. It's much more intense.'

She started getting some work from SMEs but found it hard initially. The SMEs had different mindsets, and different ways of doing business. For most of them, HR had only been a cost function. Again, she was undaunted.

'They would usually tell you that their budget was small, and would look at it from a cost point of you. The best way to convince them is to show them how these changes add value to their organization by cutting down costs and increasing productivity. You have to be able to show them the monetary benefit of the implementation of some HR policies and practices—you have to show them the rupee value.'

Over time though, Enable has gained a reputation and has a strong list of happy clients to its credit, such C.A. Galiakotwala & Co, Exim Corporation, Transasia Bio-Medicals Ltd, S&T Group Pvt. Ltd Godavari Biorefineries Ltd, Garden Silks Mills Ltd. and so on. It wasn't only the volume of work that kept increasing, but also the quality of work.

'On one of the projects I did at Godavari Sugar Mills, I got a chance to interact with the CEO and the top management. The assignment actually started off with doing job descriptions for the top three management layers, and setting some basic HR policies. As time passed, our relationship evolved into more of a partnership. They told me of their long-term plans, and asked me to do an organizational audit. I was given access to all the top executives, and was asked to talk to them. I was given a huge responsibility. I had one-on-one discussions with all of them and I had the freedom to say and ask them whatever I deemed appropriate. I had done the same in my professional career, but when you're doing it for a client and he trusts you to that extent, it's a great feeling. And that's when you know you're doing a good job.'

And that wasn't the only place where it was happening. The Garden Silk Mills, traditionally known as a fabric or a sari company, is India's second largest polyester company after Reliance. They asked Enable to do campus recruitment for them from some of India's leading B-schools.

'I was asked to represent Garden at premier B-schools. Again that was a lot of faith invested in me. I had to go to institutes such as JBIMS, where I had to handle not just the pre-process, but was entrusted with the job of taking the call on who would get the job. After a year, the responsibilities only increased with Enable doing all their HR practices, setting up their system and processes.'

This journey hasn't been without its share of difficulties.

'Doing business development initially was very tough. It was hard to get the clients and convince them that we could actually help them do better and show monetary results.'

There were some personal challenges as well. 'When you're making a shift from a corporate life to an entrepreneurial one, there has to be a shift in attitude. You have to stop being able to give yourself the option that you could go back to the corporate life whenever you hit the big roadblocks. The moment I did that, I started seeing results.'

She also feels that the entrepreneurial journey can be a lone one. 'When you're in a professional set-up, you are interacting with a lot of people; you are in a different energy space. When you are an entrepreneur you tend to become isolated. You miss that kind of interaction by being on a different track. It's important to be connected with what is happening. It's also important to see that you keep learning. In corporations you have that training and awareness level. You have people working on different things. Being an entrepreneur, especially when you are rendering a service, it's important. That's where associations and forums such as TiE—The Indus Entrepreneurs—become very important. I have learnt a lot from them.'

Falguni has always overcome these challenges through hard

work and dedication. And it certainly helps that her family is very business-oriented. Even her father is a steel trader, and her sister heads her own interior designing firm. She acknowledges her family's support throughout her career. 'My mother-in-law has stood by all my decisions and supported me all through Enable's journey. I do not need to think about my daughter when I am at office or travelling as I know she is there.'

'When I'm feeling low, I always ask my husband for advice. He is always the person I can lean on and he always motivates me. He gives me very sound advice in terms of business plans and helps me formulate the company's long-term plan. I call him Enable's Chief Financial Officer.'

This strong support from her family is backed by her faith in following sound principles at work. She believes in promising to the client only what she is capable of delivering. 'I learnt a long time back, that you should never over-promise and under-deliver, it's better to under-promise and over-deliver. That builds a consistency which always bodes well for business.'

She believes that women professionals and entrepreneurs are much more passionate and resilient in comparison to their male counterparts. Maybe, it is that passion which never fails to escape her clients. The list of clients is continuously growing and Enable is increasingly getting to partner with a lot of them on long-term strategy. 'Now there are companies where the VP-HRs themselves ask me for advice. At a number of my clients' offices, you see CEOs and the top management saying, "If Falguni is saying that we do it, we do it!"'

And with that kind of response from her clients, or 'partners' as she prefers to call them, it is hard to see Enable dong anything but scaling heights in the future. Falguni Thakkar looks set to become a role model, not only for Indian women, but to all those set to take the big leap in the world of entrepreneurship.

SUCCESS MANTRAS

'In India, I have seen that women, whether professionals or entrepreneurs, have a tendency to sell themselves a bit short. When a guy is asked to do something, his usual reply would be—"Yeah, this is so easy, I have always done it, and this is the best thing I can do," and he may never have done it in his whole life. A girl, on the other hand, would be more honest, would actually be on the defensive, and say that she has never done it, and would give it her best shot. And usually you'd see her work harder and be more successful at that job. I think women don't market themselves as well as men. We give too much credit to others and take less for ourselves. As entrepreneurs these things become more important—marketing is one of the key things you have to do, it's more important than what you do.

SATISH MANDORA
Createch Engineering, Chain Reaction,
Satellite Agrotech and Square Circles

Satish Mandora has been a man on the move. A success coach who has made a significant impact, he has experimented with ideas and ventures before discovering his true calling.

∽

CIRCLE OF LIFE

Ayush Popli and Ankit Chaturvedi

He is the perfect example of 'been there, done that'. An entrepreneur by chance, Satish Mandora is now a success coach whose profile is a combination of mentor, manager, trainer and coach who helps people utilize their potential for meaningful growth in life. What sets him apart from most others is that his life hasn't followed a conventional structure: in other words, one in which a person starts out by establishing a company and doesn't think of changing house if its foundation doesn't crumble.

Hailing from the small town of Jalgaon in Maharashtra, Satish was brought up in a traditional Marwari family that was dependent on the family business of wheat processing for their income. A few aspects that went on to define his professional life were the values that he imbibed at a young age.

Would it be right to say that hailing from a traditional Marwari business family, an MBA was always going to be a preferred career choice? Maybe not! Would it be right to say that because of his family background he had talent for business? Maybe yes!

By virtue of getting respectable scores in his 12th standard and because most of his 'friends' would stay around, he joined the College of Engineering, Pune; and pursued his graduation in Mechanical Engineering. During his engineering studies, he developed a passion for some lifelong hobbies. His friends helped him unlock many doors in his life. One such person was Praveen Joshi, who was a senior in college. They shared common interests in different activities like theatre, rowing and photography.

They became good friends. After his engineering degree, Satish decided to pursue either an M.Tech or an MBA as that was the need of the hour. To succeed in the corporate world, one requires a post-graduate degree, he thought. Satish was always aware of the fact that he did not have a penchant for engineering, though he scored well. So he applied for an MBA in Marketing at SIBM Pune. Praveen went on to pursue M.Tech at the College of Engineering, Pune.

By the end of his MBA, though Satish got placed at Bharat Petroleum, he did not feel like pursuing a corporate career whereas Praveen was working on automation of bulbs for a company. As he recollects with very fine detail, after a matinee show of Kamal Hassan's film *Appu Raja*, they went on to sit and chat at Parvati Bridge when Praveen expressed his desire to work on water fountains. The inspiration for this had come from the various water sports they used to participate in. Also, Praveen had participated in the Regatta Fest of the College of Engineering, Pune, where he had created a floating fountain in the Mula-Mutha river.

With this passion for work and an avalanche of ideas, Satish and Praveen decided to start Createch Engineering.

It is rightly said, 'It's not where you work but how you work that really matters'. This was true with this story too. They took a 40-square-feet office to start working on their new company, and their initial meetings prior to this used to be at their 'katta', as he calls it, Madhuban Café, where one of the tables next to this roadside eatery got converted into their boardroom. The initial investment was ₹256 which was used to make visiting cards.

They did not have a production facility nor did they know what their first order was (which was a nozzle), and realized that they could rent the lab facilities in College of Engineering, Pune where Praveen made the first fountain. They used the garden pipes to test it because the required pipes were not available.

Satish knew that his forte was not engineering and there was a de facto division of responsibility between the two partners. 'Pravin was the person who looked into design and production. I looked into sales and identification of markets and promoters for the product. It was teaming up of different skills required for making a wholesome experience,' he told us. Did they do any research on how to improve orders or get more business? 'Not really,' informs Satish. 'We went with our gut feeling,' he said.

Most managers would conform to the belief that you learn the art of business only when you are in it and not in the classroom. Satish had to play multiple roles at times and learn how to expand the business. They realized that government agencies such as the City and Industrial Development Corporation (CIDCO) require fountains for their parks and soon they started bagging orders for creating municipal park fountains. With the increase in orders, they finally had to recruit a maintenance engineer as well as fitters.

One memory from this venture was when they had to create the fountain at the Nerul Roundabout. 'I slept on the road for two days and I myself had to assemble the pumps and underwater lights while supervising the operations at the site,' recalls Satish fondly.

Satish got married in 1992. With the business growing and hectic work schedules, he could only visit his family during the weekends. Finally, he decided to shift to Pune with his wife and one-year-old son after his father's demise in 1996. In August 1999, he decided to move back to Jalgaon and Createch took a backseat in his life. He tried to contribute even while in Jalgaon but it got increasingly difficult owing to connectivity issues.

This was followed by an unsuccessful venture in pool tables and active entertainment. Then in 1999, Satish started a new company, Satellite Agrotech, along with his partner, Jatinder Ahluwalia. They manufactured machines for processing cereals and pulses, dust collecting systems and conveying equipment. Since then, Satellite Agrotech has become well-known in the pulse processing industry, and it still remains one of Satish's main businesses.

In his inquisitiveness to learn and develop new skills, he started attending workshops by renowned speakers. In one of the sessions given by Dr Bharat Chandra, it dawned on him that whatever he was doing in his life till now was due to chance or following a trend. This included his MBA or starting up Createch Engineering and also getting involved in his family business till the time he started Satellite Agrotech. None of these were his life choices, they all happened because of chance. He thought about his love for the stage and talking. After many restless nights, he decided to explore his passion for motivational speaking.

Satish started reading voraciously to build his knowledge. He used to visit Crossword, the bookshop, and run up bills of thousands of rupees in a single visit. He would keep attending workshops and get certifications, for which he would have to pay from his personal expenses. He got certified in Rational Emotive Behavioural Theory (REBT) and got trained at 'Nine Conversations on Leadership', in South Africa. He was also certified as a professional coach from Australia. It helped his conviction about the modules he was delivering and that they were at par with international material.

Training and development was still a very nascent concept in bigger cities like Mumbai and Pune where companies were not yet stressing a lot on skill development and employee motivation. In Jalgaon, the concept was not nascent, it was alien. Satish received a lot of flak from friends and family who told him that it was not a good idea to step back from his successfully running business and investing his time into something risky.

The training business could not support for his expenses on training programms and courses that he attended and paid from his own pocket. He was greeted by questions like: 'Koi in sab pe paise thodi na kharch karta hai!' (No one spends money on this!), 'Paagalpan hai!' (This is madness).

One of the first sessions that he conducted was a 60-minute teaser workshop for 2500 students, which was free, to attract attention to his new classes. He received only 24 registrations out of which 12 were free and 12 paid 50 per cent of the fees. But all was not lost. Even though the feedback was great, his family members were often wondering aloud if there was money to be earned in on activity like this. However, Satish wanted to expand his user base and knowledge as well as clientele even if it was for free. Any business venture would take about four years to break even and show profits

Circle of Life • 171

in the balance sheet. Satish knew that his investment in this profession was his time. The money he spent on programmes and certifications were adding to his life skills as well. So he kept on working towards his passion and added a few people to his team for business development and also a badminton pal, Tushar Chotani, as a co-trainer. Tushar would conduct training programms and also look into the area of spoken communication skills. 'Square Circles' was now a team and Manisha Panwar would add her expertise follow-through when 'real' training work started coming to them in 2009.

So how are you different? 'In enabling effective growth,' he answered. They created their flagship programme called Emotional Intelligence, which is a synthesis of training, psychometrics, follow-through and support systems. He believed that in a batch of 20 people, most trainers were able to influence almost all of them to change their habits for a brief period of time, but then they revert to their old ways in a few weeks.

'Square Circles', the organization driven by Satish, has a unique follow-through process. It follows up with the participants after the training programme to ensure that they implement the changes in their lives and keep it going. Participants responded positively by stating that they felt a change in their habits.

A big achievement for the organization was when Mahindra & Mahindra selected their flagship training programme for the organization, thanks to their progression learning and neuro-sociology. Expanding his portfolio, Satish also started conducting open workshops called 'Junoon—Passion through purpose', which helps in counselling and teaching people about the 'inside out' syndrome and how they should evolve in their life.

As we discussed ambitions for his organization, he explained that they need to go international this year and also launch an academic programme, handled by the co-trainers. He, on the other hand, would be concentrating on leadership programmes and corporate assignments. Strategic consulting and coaching small businesses has become a natural progression and they can work on measurable growth in these assignments. Kick-starting corporate meets and fuelling the drive for growth, he is invited to many forums to address them. The biggest gathering he has addressed so far was 6,500 pharmacists under a single roof.

TAKE CONTROL, BALANCE AND ENHANCE

When asked about how he balances his life so well, he said 'I firmly believe in the fact that your body can take care of you, but it cannot take care of itself. You have to take care of it, both physically and emotionally. One has to make a choice and then follow it.' He explained that it is essential to know when to say 'No'. For example, he does not stay in office after 6.30 p.m. and urges his staff to do the same. He does not take any calls during lunch and makes sure that he gets his regular dose of exercise every day.

Satish relates his habit of managing his lifestyle and professional life to his theatre experience. The rehearsals would start at 6 p.m. and continue till 4 a.m. During such times, whenever he was not practising on stage, he used to finish his journals or study for tests. This quality of multi-tasking instilled in him the ability to manage his time and ensuring the completion of his work if he has to.

While commenting on the way people should handle their lives, he maintains that he does not have any mail synchronized on his phone. The indispensability of all these devices is only in the mind of today's professionals. The challenge in today's business is that you are accountable to no one and you have to decide when to take time off to think for yourself. A very interesting concept suggested by him was that to grow your business, you should work outside your business. Only when you decongest your mind and your surroundings from the mundane work that you do, will you be able to truly think and make new decisions to grow your business.

How does someone like him get up every day and motivate himself? Essentially, how would he make others feel the same way as he does if they need to succeed in their life?

He says that he is a learner for life and every morning, he gets up with the feeling that every day is a new day and each day is going to be great. An activity that he asks all of us to do is to realize how we interact with the environment around us. It starts from the first activity in the morning with turning off the alarm, to switching off the TV in the night. Research has proved that 83 per cent of the activities that we do are because 'We have to' rather than 'We want to'. What he essentially has done has increased the 'Want to' do activities in his life which keeps him happy.

As taught to him by Swami Subodanandji, in life Utsaha = Utsav, excitement = celebration. The sources of getting Utsaha are very essential for one's physical vitality and emotional well-being. In fact, Satish's email signature is 'Celebrating Life'. This will help naturally uplift oneself and that's when Emotional Quotient will be equal to Spiritual Quotient.

His learning comes from diverse sources. Dealing with people and their inner world is very different. Although the principles are the same, the individual experience and beliefs are quite diverse. His inner world, unless touched, will not take in the learnings. This is where connecting with ground realities becomes essential. For working with a sales team, you have to go to the retailer and listen to what is said about them that they do not listen to. Customizing each solution and connecting with reality can only happen by researching and interacting a lot on the topic or the subject matter. To him, all these areas appear interconnected because Satish as a trainer is also Satish as a father, as a son, as a brother, as a friend, as an industry professional and a vagabond who loves to enjoy life in different ways. The lifetime learning trait is a 'non-negotiable' value, he concludes. He feels fortunate to have learnt from more than 15,000 (now 30,000) participants he has interacted with, and at the end of every session, the only question he asks himself is 'Who learnt the most out of this, the participants or I?'

Looking back, Satish also realizes that the strong support provided by his elder brother Kishor, in taking care of the basic family necessities, did not let the pressure build on him. Thanks to the close-knit family, the strong sense of values in stilled by his mother, Yashoda, the cordial exchange between the ladies of the family, namely, his bhabhi Varshali and wife Mitu, who live more like sisters than sisters-in-law, he could concentrate on his work.

SUCCESS MANTRAS

One key learning from his experience is that customers will always be ready to work with you for three simple reasons:
a) Commitment
b) Trust
c) Never avoid them even if you are not fulfilling a commitment.

To all those who intend to follow the same path as Satish, his advice is that great conversation and presentation skills alone don't amount to success as a motivational speaker. 'We are talking about human lives; it could be very dangerous what kind of effects it could have, if not properly understood. What is really essential is to have a very high standard of work ethics and practice what you preach,' he says.

To become a great success coach, you have to keep learning continuously and feel good about life. Fundamentally, you need to exemplify the virtues of a 'good human'.

AHMED FAIYAZ
Grey Oak Publishers India Pvt. Ltd

An MBA and a qualified chartered accountant, Ahmed Faiyaz has floated his own publishing house and also writes stories for his numerous readers. Now, that's an unusual story.

∽

WORDS' WEAVER

Dhruvish Thakkar and Varun Tejwani

Ahmed Faiyaz wears many hats. He is a qualified CA who, after starting his career with the company KPMG, quit his job to pursue his MBA. He is currently working as a consultant in Dubai, has authored some of the bestsellers in India and is a publisher as well. He's a strategist by profession, with a number of years in management consulting behind him. He's a book and film addict. Apart from reading books and watching films of all genres, he is a passionate writer. His first book, *Love, Life and All That Jazz...*' published in April 2010 was a popular bestseller across major cities. He is also one of the founding members of Grey Oak Publishers which released *Another Chance*, his second, bestselling full-length novel. He has also contributed stories to the bestselling *Urban Shots*. He enjoys long getaways in the mountains or to secluded beaches, where he reads a book a day. Moreover, he reviews books for *Asian Age*, *Helter Skelter* and *The Tossed Salad*. He's also the co-editor of *Down the Road*.

The best place to meet an author is at a bookstore. So we decided to catch Ahmed at one of his book launches at a Crossword outlet in Phoenix Market City, Pune. We see a huge bunch of young and enthusiastic readers eagerly waiting for the launch to begin. Not much later, a young guy who appears to be around 30 years of age enters the scene. He is wearing spectacles while a warm smile is playing hide-and-seek on his face. It is difficult to imagine that this young man who is dressed in a regular striped shirt and a pair of jeans is the person we had been waiting for.

It is when he starts talking to his admirers that his perceptive mind unfolds in full public view. Well-equipped with his knowledge about marketing and management, he keeps his audience engaged by showcasing excerpts from the book in the form of short video films, facilitating discussions and addressing all the questions very well. After the eventful and exciting launch comes to an end, Ahmed sits down to share his story with us over a few cups of coffee.

Raised in Bangalore, once a sleepy old pensioner's paradise, Ahmed had a very productive childhood. On asking about his childhood interests, Ahmed recalls, 'Where do I begin? For as long as I remember, I have always wanted to write. I guess the journey begins from reading books at an early age. I have been a voracious reader as a child. I began by reading comics like *Tintin* and *Asterix* while also devouring the weekly dose of *Tinkle, Archie* and Superhero comics (*Batman, The Green Lantern* and *Spiderman* in particular). My parents encouraged me to keep reading. By the time I turned eight, I had read children's classics versions of *Tom Sawyer, Oliver Twist, Moby Dick, A Tale of Two Cities* and *The Adventures of Huckleberry Finn*. I soon moved on to *Ukrainian Tales* (A hardbound 500+ pages collection of short stories) which my dad had picked up for me.'

'I was also privileged to have the membership of two libraries close to home. At the end of every week, my parents would take me down to one or both libraries to borrow books in which I would lose myself all weekend. My mum also brought me books which she believed I should read from her school's library, where she was a member, starting with the full range of *Noddy* books at the age of five; *Aesop's Fables* a year later and classics like *Robinson Crusoe* a couple of years after that. I would finish reading my English Literature textbook on the day when all textbooks were given out, a week prior to the start of a school year. After finishing this, I would go and borrow my cousin Ibrahim's (three years older in the same school) textbooks and finish this too. Often my brother and I went over to our cousin Roshini Anand's home to play or watch cassettes of animated films. I remember spending most of my time in front of her bookshelf, taking out one book after another and finishing them.' No wonder Ahmed's early start coupled with his parent's encouraging support laid the foundation for a bestselling author-to-be.

A writer usually seeks inspiration from well-established names in the field, but not Ahmed. Talking about his childhood inspiration, he says 'I guess one looks up to people in one's surrounding, and in my case, I had a deep admiration for my Nana, who was a wonderful human being. He passed away a few months after I finished my MBA at SIBM. Co-incidentally he was a failed entrepreneur who ended up managing his cousin's business for over 25 years before he left to help my uncle set up a chain of restaurants. He was over 70 then. What makes him my role model was his belief in integrity and honesty, the goodwill he built around him, the way he conducted himself. He was an impeccable gentleman and had a mild-mannered nature but was a strict disciplinarian both at work and at home. I also looked up to my dad who was an entrepreneur from the age of 14 till he passed away at the age of 54. In between he managed businesses for others, but he was at his best being his own boss. My uncle who passed out from IIT and did his MBA at Kellogg is also a source of inspiration and continues to be a role model. He runs a mid-sized IT Services company in New Jersey.'

As a kid, Ahmed Faiyaz was never too ambitious. He was not a seeker of money or fame. He was a bit of a dreamer and loved to read. He applied himself quite well at studies. 'I didn't work too hard in school but managed to stay within the top percentile. I always waited for exams to end so I could get back to reading, playing tennis and other interests. I picked up things quickly, especially Maths and Science subjects, and that gave me breathing space to do other things such as read, write, act and direct little plays and get involved with extracurricular activities. I wish I had more of that, but those were fun times.'

Inspired by his uncle who runs an IT set-up, he enrolled in a six-month course at the NIIT while doing his B.Com. 'I thought maybe I could extend that into a two-year course if I took to it. I didn't take to it, and ended up discontinuing it after six months. It was a bit of fun to learn something new but I couldn't imagine doing it for the rest of my life.' He then heeded the advice of another uncle who is a successful chartered accountant and decided to give that a shot. This he did, and he went through with it with some difficulty. Two years into it, he just wanted to get his degree and check out, as being an auditor or someone working with numbers or becoming a banker didn't quite excite or inspire him. 'I felt that I was the ideas guy. I wanted new things to do each time and realized I would enjoy taking on different challenges and situations. This is what steered me into an MBA in Marketing and a career in consulting which laid the foundation to do my own thing.'

It was while he was working at KPMG that he took an important decision. Leaving a well-paying job for pursuing an MBA was not easy for Ahmed. He fondly remembers, 'I put in my papers at KPMG and walked out for a chat with the Senior Manager while he took his smoke break. He was quite fond of me and advised me against it, saying that if I changed boats midstream, I would run the risk of sinking in the process. But I guess he was proved wrong as a few others followed in my footsteps. I feel an MBA is a holistic learning process. A lot depends on your approach to it during those two years. I saw some people come in and go out as the same people without any growth or sense of who they are and what they want to be. But I think I grew a lot as a person during those two years, apart from sharpening my skills and figuring out what I was good at.'

Finally, Ahmed gave his passion for writing a chance, eventually leading him to his entrepreneurial venture: publishing. 'Writing a book is something I wanted to do for years but it seemed impossible given the busy life at work. In 2009, I finally moved to a role which offered me a balanced lifestyle, where I could get home at a certain time and have my weekends, which then led to the challenge of sitting down and giving it a shot. It was difficult getting started, given that this was something completely new and required a different sort of focus and discipline.' In March 2010, Ahmed's first novel *Love, Life and All That Jazz* was released which went on to become a bestseller which was followed up quickly by *Another Chance*, another bestseller. Ahmed embraced glory at a very young age in his life. For Ahmed, publishing is something that happened by accident. The idea kind of grew out of his first publishing experience with a small set-up based in Delhi which was frustrating at best. He felt there was so much more that a publisher could do, and he realized that he could do it himself, considering that most publishers work through their existing networks and close their doors to those outside the cliques. The opportunity was clear as there were heaps of capable writers waiting to get published while the number of quality publishers was very limited, focused mostly on literary fiction and not mass market fiction. While, he was at the Jaipur Literature Festival, he met a number of writers who had experiences similar to his. It also gave him some sense of how publishers functioned and made him realize that there was enough opportunity for others to enter this space and make a success of it. Thus was born Grey Oak Publishers India Pvt. Ltd.

Like any other entrepreneurial venture, the initial days were very tough for Grey Oak Publishers. 'We had a lot of teething troubles from getting ISBN numbers issued to getting our website up in time and getting initial orders for our titles. We were nobody then and there was no reason for big bookstores to commit their budgets to our titles,' Ahmed explains. The solution to this problem was the biggest lesson that MBA taught him: networking. He explains, 'I had built up a few contacts with key bookstores and people in the trade with my first book. Those relationships really helped us move forward and gain acceptances as initial orders were sought on the strength of my name and the success of my first book.'

Talking about Grey Oak Publishers, Ahmed explains, 'J.K. Rowling submitted *Harry Potter* to 12 publishing houses, all of which rejected it. Margaret Mitchell's *Gone with the Wind* was faced with rejection 38 times. She won a Pulitzer Prize in 1937 for her book. *Carrie* by Stephen King was rejected over 30 times before being published. The novel became a classic in the horror genre.' One can surely find such examples a dime a dozen in the industry. In our very own country, there is so much talent which never gets a chance to showcase its potential. Thanks to Ahmed, several new authors have achieved literary fame as well. He has a knack of identifying new talent and nurturing it. Grey Oak Publishers gives him the opportunity of being small but relevant. He is consistently bringing new authors to the market and is extremely happy to see their proud faces at book launches. And he is doing this by publishing books that people love and want to read. He has not just achieved glory for himself but helped others achieve it as well. And that is what true entrepreneurship is all about.

An MBA is definitely a boost to one's corporate career but its importance for entrepreneurship always invokes different opinions. Ahmed explains, 'I don't think it's absolutely necessary, but it's certainly good to have. I believe that the difference is in the journey and not in whether you have a degree or a placement or not. These things stop mattering a few months after your MBA. What does matter is what you've learned, the things you've been through, the things you've got done and the different types of people you've worked with. It certainly is a good place to start if one wants to cut one's teeth in the real world trying to build a business. I believe it helps tremendously as you are able to look at a scenario from different angles, look at the bigger picture and try to work through a network of relationships and set-ups in the chain. I don't think any other qualification prepares you to run a business more than an MBA does.'

He has never felt like quitting even in the toughest of times. He has a special mention for the strong moral support backing him everywhere and every time, particularly his mum and his brother. 'Whenever I feel down, I just pick up the phone and talk to my mum, my brother or a close friend.'

About balancing professional life with personal life, he says 'It certainly isn't easy as what you're doing is your baby and you have to support it all times. It's a 24/7 job'. His advice is—'Do it if you love it as only then you will be able ride through the long hours and get things done while having a sense of satisfaction in what you do. There were a number of opportunities to start-up, ranging from cafés to restaurants with friends and business associates in Bangalore and Pune but I didn't quite get excited by any of these as you must do it only if you love it.'

Also, one remarkable thing about his venture is that he has not met with any failures till date. All the books of Grey Oak Publishers to date have been successful. Some failures, according to Ahmed, have been terminations of relationships with a few designers, editors and distributors. But then it's a part and parcel of doing business. He goes on, 'It's best to complete what you're doing together and part ways amicably.'

Just a week before we interviewed him, *'Urban Shots'—Crossroads* which he contributed to and edited, and *'Scammed'—Confessions of a Confused Accountant*, both made it to the top 10 national bestsellers across India. At such an early stage in life, Ahmed owns a publishing company and has titles to his name either as a writer or as an editor. Ahmed does attribute his success to luck and God but firmly believes that nothing would have been possible in the absence of self-belief, dedication and commitment.

Ahmed's plans for future are to be successful at what he does. Most importantly, he wants to ensure that everyone involved with his projects is happy. Also, he plans to spend a lot more time with his family, especially his son. 'These days my baby inspires me. He is a joy to hang out with. There's never a dull moment with him.'

SUCCESS MANTRAS

'Most businesses are built on a network of relationships.

Your business needs to adapt itself to the changing environment.

Have belief, dedication and commitment.

When the going gets tough, the tough get going.'

KHODABAD IRANI
High Spirits Café

A maverick who ran pubs and discos before starting out on his own, Khodabad Irani has experienced a high with High Spirits, his own joint with a touch of difference. Competitors will come and go, but none can take its place in Pune's nightlife.

༄

KING OF HIGH

Team SIBM

If you ever come to Pune, one thing you'd never want to miss is its happening nightlife. And one of the major players in this scene is Khodabad Irani aka Khodu. A young and zealous entrepreneur, Khodu started his journey with his first venture—The Dream Theatre, an event management company, while he was still pursuing his MBA. After running pubs and discos for others, he hoped to create a place with a different touch when compared to clubs or the run-of-the-mill bars. With this intent, he opened the 'High Spirits Café' in 2006. High Spirits most certainly pioneered the way for unconventional theme nights in restaurants. With great music and something different happening every week, High Spirits boasts of a very loyal clientele.

A fun guy to talk to, Khodu had a liberal upbringing in Pune's upmarket Koregaon Park. After finishing his schooling from St Vincent's High School and his junior college from the Wadias, he joined the MBA programme at SIBM Pune. Reminiscing about his childhood days, Khodu says, 'Pune, back then, was not a big city as it is today. Staying in Koregaon Park, I knew most of the people. Koregaon Park in those days was like a global village because of the Rajneesh Ashram. We had foreigners coming down from all across the globe. We used to have a bungalow and an outhouse where we had foreigners coming and staying for months. I guess I shaped my perspective in those days, because of the vivid influences from all around the place.'

Khodu, since his childhood days, was a fun-loving chap. 'I didn't really think a lot about my goals and plans back then. For me, most of the time, it was just about having fun—get through school, do lots of *masti*, play sports. I loved sports and that kept me active most of the times. I was a jack of all trades and master of none. After clearing my SSC, I want to get out of school. By the time I got to HSC, I wanted to get out of it. Then it was just party time. So at that point, I really did not think about my career. Moreover, during those days, one did not have many career options like today. MBA was one of the coveted and promising careers to opt for. That was how it worked for me.'

Back then, his family used to have a bakery. Spotting that there was no fast food place in that area, he immediately sprang into action and converted it into one. He also planned on starting a pool parlour. Contrary to the visionaries and great entrepreneurs whom a lot of us have looked up to, Khodu embodies the idea of how one can be a small yet innovative entrepreneur and still be happy.

Khodu tells us, 'Always it was kind of about entrepreneurship but different kinds of entrepreneurship. I was doing something what other people were not doing, but in a different way. I have always liked interacting with people and that is where my ideas have revolved around.'

When asked why he wanted to do an MBA, Khodu is typically forthright. 'I did an MBA because I needed a degree.

However, he doesn't dismiss the MBA experience entirely. 'I learnt much more by doing the extracurricular activities in Symbiosis than in my class. In fact, my first exposure to the corporate world was when I was asked to get sponsorship for an event at college. Besides, one's background, the marketing talk, all that helps to smoothen the teething troubles.'

That background helped Khodu since his business relied on him marketing it well. 'This business is 90 per cent word-of-mouth,' insists Khodu. 'Early on, at that time it was more of a hand-to-mouth existence. We were not about the money; we were not earning big bucks or anything.' While High Spirits Café might have been conceptualized when he was young, he had no shortage of experience. 'At that time, I had almost run every bar in Pune. Soon after, I realized that I have learnt enough to start my own place. Finally, when I was sure how to run a restro-bar, I decided to start one myself.

'We started out pretty small. I'd borrowed money from my parents. But this isn't like a traditional space. I did the interiors myself. Over time what I realized was that it's not how the place looks but the energy of the place and the people who come that matter. I started out just as a retro-bar. We were doing retro music, Tuesday to Sunday. There were no events, only different DJs playing music. At that time, around the country, clubs were doing new things. I was the first person to do something like that in Pune. Tuesdays we started doing karaoke, Wednesdays we started doing open nights, Thursdays bladder bursts, which everybody started ripping off. Fridays we have live acts, covering the best live acts across the country. We also keep doing innovative theme parties. Basically, what we started, people are aping all across the country. We basically were the first movers.'

Thus, in spite of numerous difficulties, Khodu was able to give shape to his entrepreneurial career while still in college, thus living the dream of every MBA graduate. At that time, his friend and he started out as promoters; it was just about promoting a place and at the same time, getting to know the business, the market, making friends, what people want, what their needs are and how does one make it interesting for a person, what made the customers choose a select few over the others, and other factors. After getting such insight, they realized that, as promoters they were getting only 10 per cent of the cut whereas the bar owners used to keep the rest. So they played a little smart, and started doing farm parties. They started renting out farms, getting their own music systems, their own bouncers, and started doing parties there. With that they slowly started to progress. Later, to build some equity in the market and to win the hearts of a larger audience, Khodu started organizing some quality events with the older crowd. They did the Zaakir Hussain show, Pune dance festival, Shaniwarwada dance festival and others. which were targeted to a much wider audience.

Khodu insists that the business is about love, and cautions against entering a business only to make profits, unlike a lot of companies today that believe that 'Profit is the only reality'. 'At that point in time, there was no money. The money was in corporate events or weddings. But we did not want to be wedding planners. There is a huge amount of money in weddings even today. But that was not our aim in life. We liked being creative, we liked having fun. There were a lot of ways, we could have made money, like taking up a corporate job, but that wouldn't serve our purpose. Even during my summer internship with L'Oreal, I did a couple of events for them. We conceptualized hair shows for them, which has become a norm in the market today.'

Being a second-generation entrepreneur might lead one to believe that Khodu was encouraged in his endeavours, but that does not appear to be the case. 'In fact, my dad thought I was wasting time doing parties, events etc. He wasn't too happy that I was doing such stuff. But I always wanted to do something different, and when I look back, I am proud that I am doing something on my own. I started working when I was 17 years old. In the day I used to do tiffin service, which was a family run business and in the evening, I used to work at Levis. At that time, the MNCs had just started coming in and Levis was one of the first ones. It was kind of the coolest place to work. I was working at ₹800 a month at that time. That managed to give me a very good practical exposure at a very young age.'

So what was his family's reaction when he began his venture? 'My mum was always very supportive. My dad was more into the traditional forms of business, so he wasn't too comfortable with the creative side of handling business. I used to wake up every day at 12 o'clock in the afternoon and get nagged by him, but slowly he saw that I was working and putting in effort. As I started progressing, he became more comfortable. And in business, its 90 per cent hard work, 10 per cent luck. In anything you do, you have to slog.'

That philosophy of 'slogging' is supported by Khodu's intense desire to constantly innovate and improve his offerings. 'Life is a learning experience, so you never stop learning. Even today, when I am going abroad, I am checking out stuff. A lot of people stop at a particular point and say this is it, but you should always keep learning. The more you go out and speak to the public, the more you learn. So that time, it was a good experience. While selling jeans, you have to convince a customer that he is looking good, the fit is perfect and so on. That helps you build your communication skills. If you are a sales person, you can converse with anybody.'

Khodu re-emphasizes the luck aspect, and how it helped High Spirits Café in its initial stages. 'At my time, it wasn't so competitive. But slowly, it started getting more tough. Today, if I were to start a new place, it will be crazy. Even for me, to go back and start something today wouldn't be easy. Starting up is challenging and its fun. I literally started from scratch, from nothing, and it takes hard work.'

So having begun High Spirits, Khodu now needed to rope in the best performers of the day to ensure that people visited his café. Did he find it daunting? 'Not really. As I was already involved in the Pune Festival, I was quite comfortable while handling big celebrities. I knew that at the end of the day even they are humans. After a while it becomes a job, like just another job. You handle people, their tantrums and get things done. But mainly you enjoy it because you're getting to meet such kind of people. You get to build contacts.'

Khodu insists that maintaining relationships is the key to running a successful enterprise. Out of the 200–250 odd people he expects, he personally knows 100–150 people. 'People like it when you treat them well. And our tagline is "Come home to the high". So we try to make our customers feel at home when they are here. It's important to make them feel wanted. It makes a big difference.'

The story of High Spirits Café isn't as smooth as one would think, however, and Khodu Irani has experienced his share of failures. 'I experience failures all the time. When I started out, I did not have a licence for one year. We had to stick out there, wait for the licence to come in. So we hardly had any business for the first year. I used to take a one-day licence for Sunday and used to run the place only on Sundays. After that, there were no approach roads, and we had issues for parking, so we got that arranged. There is a continuous struggle in this line. There are constant failures. There are days when you are not doing any business. You have to keep at it. There is no point when you can let go. You cannot slacken. In a month I'm almost here for 23 days, mornings and evenings. You cannot just let it go. We used to arrange parties for 700–800 people. I could have continued doing that. But I downsized, because I realized I am happy doing this, and I did not want the additional stress. I decided on a particular amount that I wanted to earn and stuck to that. You have to handle so many different types of taxes. It's madness.'

High Spirits Café is the most loved venue for most of the café's performers. 'I think there's a video online. If you can check it out on YouTube, just check out High Spirits Cafe. They've all spoken about it, and basically the kind of vibes they get from the crowd. They just don't get it anywhere else. People say this is their favourite venue to perform. Vir Das only wants to perform here in Pune. If he has a choice, he'd prefer only High Spirits. So most of the bands, they prefer it here, I don't even pay them the kind of money that other places pay them but the kind of vibe, the response they get from the crowd makes the place special.'

As of now, Khodu has no plans to expand High Spirits Café into a chain. 'I have received offers, but I don't really want to put my foot into something I'm not sure about. I want to do it the right way. I don't want to just start it for the money. I didn't do High Spirits for the money. Even if you see today, I sell a beer for 120 bucks. When you go to a dhaba today, a beer costs you 120 bucks.

'I'm looking at expanding, but not right now. I don't want to do such a thing in this field because this is a full-time occupation. You don't have any family life, you're here in the morning, and you're here at night. This becomes your life. You have no time for anything else. When you have children, coming home in the wee hours I don't know if I want to do that. If you're in a job, you might be out for 20 days. But at least if you're at home for five days, then you're there with your kids. When you're on leave you're on leave. Here you don't have any offs like that. I went for my honeymoon in September one year after I got married. So it's quite a hectic life.'

He says that this business is not a science, it's an art. So one cannot make many systems. It's the personal touch, the warmth that makes a difference. Just because a restaurant is doing well doesn't mean all restaurants will do well the same way.

'You've got to be calm, you've got to always smile all the time, and you've got to be happy all the time and serve with a smile. And you have to be intuitive because you've got to know what people like.'

SUCCESS MANTRAS

'Follow your dream. There will be a lot of hardships. Unless you go out there and start doing it, you will never know whether you could have achieved it or not.

'A lot of people have an idea, but they don't do the core basic work behind it. Their idea is good, but how to implement that idea, get it off the ground, and how to sustain it and take it to the next level is what is important. Hence, plan thoroughly.'

NISHANT PARASHAR
engage4more (I) Pvt. Ltd

From struggle to success: few can epitomize this as well as Nishant Parashar does. As he heads a leading employee engagement company, his is a story of what such a long journey actually means.

☽

RULES OF ENGAGEMENT

Amit Kr. Chand and Yogesh Agarwal

His USP is engage4more, India's leading employee engagement company providing integrated services in events, content, technology and consultancy. An intrepid entrepreneur with a bestselling idea, Nishant Parashar and his organization have received numerous awards. Among them are the Businessworld Hottest Young Entrepreneur Award 2011, Emerging Company of the Year at the Economic Development Forum 2011, Star Start-up of the Year by the Indira Institute of Management, Pune 2012, and Silver at ABEC awards for the anniversary film produced for IDFC Ltd 2013. Besides, he has also been nominated for ET Now Leaders of Tomorrow 2012.

Statistics tell the whole story. Within a short span of three years, engage4more has helped in creating engagement for over 20,00,000 employees in more than 90 large cap organizations. These include some of the world's leading corporate houses like Reliance Industries, TCS, Capita, Standard Chartered, HSBC, Dow, Sanofi, Abbott, RBS, IDFC, AegonReligare, Tata AIG, HDFC ERGO, HUL, PernodRicard, Disney, Nielsen, ACG Worldwide, Godrej, Vodafone, MCX, Linkedin and Eli Lilly, to name a few. It also produces and promotes CTC (Corporate Talent Championship), a performing arts platform in music, acting, dancing and singing. With over 120 corporates participating, CTC is the world's largest inter-corporate platform. Besides delivering on employee engagement and employer branding priorities, CTC also promotes living values at work and diversity and inclusion for differently abled people.

It has been a short but outstanding journey for Nishant, who did his schooling from Delhi, engineering from Haryana and MBA from SIBM Pune. He had what he says is a 'very humble, hardworking, values-oriented middle class family upbringing.' His father, Jai Bhagwan Parashar, is an ex-navy, ex-excise and taxation inspector, and his mother, Leela Vati Parashar, is presently a school teacher in Delhi. There was an entrepreneurial spark in him since his early days in engineering, and the seed of event management was sown by organizing a inter-university festival on his own.

Reflecting on his life, he admits that the festival proved to be a turning point in his life. 'It decided the direction for the journey this far and beyond. I did my engineering from Deen Bandhu Chhotu Ram University of Science and Technology in Haryana, which at that time was culturally dead. The curious and fun-loving group I belonged to obviously wasn't going to settle for that. From my first year itself, we started going out and performing at almost all cultural festivals in north India. Suddenly, in my second year, the idea of doing an inter-college fest in my own college came up. For a college which wasn't that known and culturally active, that was an insane thought. It was like India dreaming of hosting a football World Cup. Many more friends joined in. After two years of hard work, which included visiting all college festivals (participating and inviting colleges), losing attendance and somehow managing to appear in exams, going to retail shops and industrial areas to raise sponsorship, staying back in the hostel while all others were enjoying their vacations, we managed to pull off the very first inter-college festival in our college.'

'Around 20 universities participated, and over 3000 students came over. This fest was organized in my final year (fourth year of engineering). We lost a lot of money and body mass but surely identified where passion wanted me to go further. My friends told me that what I did during the whole of my college days was actually called "event management" and a potential industry in the making.'

In a turn of events, during a development session at SIBM while he was doing his MBA, a gentleman from Percept was present. In an interaction with the person, Nishant managed to impress him. The person told Parashar, 'You are focused and I would like you to meet my CEO, Sanjay Lal.' He swiftly replied, 'Sir, I would like to do an internship with you as well.'

Some may call it luck, but only an entrepreneur would call it an opportunity—the way Nishant utilized the situation to get an internship offer for himself was extraordinary. After the internship, it was time for placements. He recalls, 'I wanted to join a Times of India Group company called 360 Degrees. These guys were doing a rock show in Pune. I didn't know whom to ask to get a job. People made fun of me—'*Tu engineering and MBA karke kya event karega?* (How will you do event management after doing engineering and MBA?)'

Somehow, after two long months, he got an appointment. He was offered a job with a salary of ₹8000. He would have accepted the job for half the salary. So he happily took it up. He continues, 'I joined as an executive. The next year I was a

Manager and the year after that, I was an Event Manager and then I was the Group Manager. All this within three and a half years. I got salary increments like 80 per cent, 95 per cent, 85 per cent and 67 per cent back to back, which was never heard of in a TOI Group company.'

In 2006, he left 360 Degrees where he was working on corporate events, concerts, weddings, seminars, launches, PR events, press conferences and so on. And then Standard Chartered Bank happened. Reflecting on these two jobs, he says, 'I had a great mix of selling and buying experience before founding engage4more because of my selling and servicing stint at 360 Degrees where I delivered in over 100-plus corporate events besides seeing large events like Filmfare and Femina very closely followed by my stint at Standard Chartered Bank where I used to look after corporate brand, sponsorship and internal communications besides heading the corporate affairs function for Mauritius. These two stints offered high quality exposure that gave me both sides' perspective, and more importantly, exposed the mighty gaps between expectations and delivery. While working on the Standard Chartered Mumbai Marathon, I got stimulated by the art of engaging a city and communities which comes in handy in creating employee engagement solutions for super-large corporates. These two stints also exposed me to the largest possibilities of the nation and beyond which has immensely contributed to my knowledge and also aspirations.'

So was corporate life as hunky dory as it seems? He admits to some failures at corporate life, 'Not all my projects have done wonders. In Standard Chartered Bank, I, along with my agency had not done the right calculations on space and planning for one of very crucial events. I could see the crowd. I could see the filth. I could see the chaos and confusion. That has been the darkest day of my career. I am very optimistic and ambitious but I am very conscious of failures. That very same project, we did with world-class execution and unparalleled participation from employees one year later.'

When asked whether his entrepreneurship was an accident or a planned one, he says, 'Definitely it's not an accident. It has happened to me very naturally. I have done engineering and MBA. Lots of my homework was done there itself. I could figure out who my competitors are and what they do.'

Though it looks terrific now, it wouldn't have been easy to zero in on what engage4more should offer. He acknowledges that and recalls that there is a huge market gap mainly because everyone sells products, not value. Thus, the idea that he would sell value started shaping up. He made some simple calculations like he would do business in the country with the largest working population. Thus, engage4more was created in India. Currently, the company aims at only large capital companies with ₹1000 crore-plus revenue and 500-plus employees. These are multinationals because they are the guys who understand the significance of engagement.

How would he define engagement? He explains it very simply, 'Engagement starts at a very basic level. If one is talking to a person's father, wife or son, one has to strike the right chord with all of them. This is where organizations go wrong. They have to reach out to their employees, sometimes as a friend, mentor, sometimes as a kid, as a teacher and so on. We bring in the basics of how a wedding is organized, where each and every guest is very important. Likewise, each and every employee on board is very important.'

Today, Prashant has a cracked a unique code which attracts prominent clients. He informs us about what his organization does. 'We provide a heterogeneous mix of services ranging from research, events, internal communication, advertising, merchandizing, software building, along with mind-mapping tools, colour therapy solutions, pottery workshops, and even sex education workshops. There are also many other services like providing library services, photography workshops, or marriage management. At engage4more we do all of this and more.'

Nishant feels that to engage an employee, there cannot be one single consideration. An employee is not engaged only because of the salary. There are eight different factors resulting in employee engagement:

1. Money
2. Means
3. Ownership
4. Objective
5. Role
6. Recognition
7. Emotional connect
8. Enjoyment

He also believes that there is a lot of pride in being an Indian company. 'India has a huge problem of a lack of a skilled workforce. A suitable candidate who had three offers last year will have eight offers next year. This means that employee branding as a subject would become very, very popular. A company will have to become very attractive so that somebody says "Boss, I have to join this company." If you thought Tata was a big deal in Tata Motors, a Volkswagen entering and selling becomes a change. So everything that Tata offered has now become a base. Secondly, when people have joined you, how do you constantly engage them? Things are changing so fast. So there is a talent war. We help companies fight that war.'

To elaborate, he says, 'The real job is to understand your company and your employee—what their behaviour is and what it will take to engage them as human beings—and put that in the workplace. So it could be about creating an iPad application for a CEO and at the same time, initiating a "bhajan-kirtan" competition for the peon. If you are a McKinsey guy, I'll provide library services for you. If I am doing a sports event, I will try to engage a pregnant woman by making her play Sudoku or chess. These are our fundamentals—we believe in inclusive engagement.'

An entrepreneur needs to always keep it going by means of setting a benchmark for himself and his team. 'Opening a letter itself becomes an experience. So Steve Jobs would sit and work on opening the box experience of an iPod, iPad, et al. This is a very different delight altogether. When he called people to join, he didn't say it's a job, he said "it's a calling." He's been a revolution and he is my role model.' Apart from Jobs, his other inspiration comes from Google. 'The technology called Psychic search predicts what you are going to enter. Whenever Google launches anything, I carefully follow it.'

But all these are external forces. There has to be fuel that helps you light the burner. And there has to be a spark that ignites it. Here is the incident that sparked Nishant's life. 'My mother had a paralysis attack while in a train six years ago. After one and half hours at 6.30 a.m., my father got to know about it. We were deciding on where the ambulance should take her.

Somebody said that Max Hospital had neurosurgeons who were the best. Fortunately, we were lucky to get her treated in time.' It was one of those episodes that has taught Parashar a lot.

As time goes by, Parashar would like to bring a lot of technology to engage people. 'I believe technology can be a big thing in changing the world. It's about fundamentals. Look at Facebook. Mark Zuckerberg understands technology and human behaviour. Our need is to be connected as we are social animals. I believe we can connect with technology also. There are lots of plans to use the power of technology to create an engaged workforce.'

He further adds to his future plans—

- 'We have a very busy life. We don't have time to worry about car insurance, electricity bill, et al. Imagine if I have a back office that takes care of all these things. It's not a new concept. We always believe in connecting better—this way, the employees would get more time to do things that they want to do.
- Another thing we are currently looking at is an Emergency BPO concept. As a corporate what you are looking for is a BPO which takes care of all your emergencies.'

Networking, according to him, is of huge significance for an entrepreneur. He says, 'References are important. In B2B, word of mouth is extremely important. Also, social media like Facebook, LinkedIn community, database, adds a lot to public campaign. All these are critical.' He adds, 'People should know me for my integrity, sincerity and passion. I was able to do double the work asked because of my sincerity. I tell people either you are a labourer or a creator. A labourer is one who does what is told to him and a creator is one who modifies it or creates something new. So my intensity lies in the creation.'

'There are those who have played a crucial role in my life: my wife, my in-laws and my parents. My wife had shown great support. My parents were not sure, but they knew that I would end up doing something good. My in-laws have a business in Pune. So when I explained my concept to them, they were satisfied and gave me an encouraging response.'

SUCCESS MANTRAS

'Lead: What got you here won't help you tomorrow. Lead your client. Lead your vendors, lead your team. You need to check whether you are leading or being led. Leading has a very great value. You always check which quartile you are in.

Surprise: Keep innovating in the way you created things, the way you sold, the way you structured the deal, how you ran a campaign...

ROTI (Return on Time Investment): Respect people's time and your own time. Ask for money according to the time you are spending. Justify your time. Also value your client's time. Work in a team for better time utilization.'

RAJSHRI GOLE
The Catalyst

Every company needs employees with specific skills that address its needs. This requirement inspired Rajshri Gole, who is now a successful HR entrepreneur, to provide quality recruitment solutions.

☙

SHE FILLS IN THE BLANKS

Team SIBM

Some things happen without notice. An MBA from SIBM who had taken a break and also undergone a surgery, Rajshri Gole had an idea one day. She knew that it had potential. What she needed to do was take it forward and make it happen. That, she did, the result being that Rajshri runs a successful HR firm with a twist today.

The lady who hails from a typical Maharastrian family has been in Pune for as long as she can remember. Her father worked for All India Radio and was transferred every three years. For most of her childhood, Rajshri stayed with her relatives in Pune. They took very good care of her, not just out of love but also out of a huge sense of responsibility. All in all, they were very protective of her. This had made her very secluded from the rest of the society. With little scope for outdoor games, she turned to reading and more importantly, to music. Music has stayed with her to this date as her favorite hobby. As a child, she never dreamt of being an entrepreneur, not even of working in the domain of business or management.

Two years later she was out of college and working on a sales assignment for a period of 11 months. During this time, she was able to treble the sales volume. Post this assignment, she moved on to a corporate sales role where she was expected to deal in securing cab rental contracts from corporates. During these two initial assignments, she learned the tricks of the trade and gained a lot of confidence. At one point she felt that she could sell anything to almost anyone! It was during this time that she had her first thoughts of starting an entrepreneurial venture.

It was only during her third job at CIFCO Finances that she finally got to do what she really dreamed of doing post-MBA—financial marketing. While working here she got several opportunities to meet the who's who of Pune. She got married in 1993 and when the Harshad Mehta scam came to light, all hell broke loose. CIFCO was owned by Bhupen Dalal, who was one of those involved with Harshad Mehta in the financial scam of early 1980s. That was when she was asked to do recoveries. Financial marketing was one thing and recovering money from parties a completely different ballgame. However, not willing to give up, she stuck to her task and went from office to office doing recoveries too!

After her third job, she had a child and took a break from work for about a year. She had also undergone a surgery during that period. It was during this sabbatical that she had to decide whether to go back and get a regular job again or start something of her own. She had the same doubts that every mother would have about her child—how to manage time for the child during weekdays, who would take care of the child during her absence and other similar concerns.

The idea for her entrepreneurial venture came to her quite by chance. One day at her sister's place, who is also working in the field of Human Resources, she chanced upon some CVs lying around. She asked her sister what these CVs were for.

She was told that they were rejects and nothing could be done about them. But Rajshri was looking at the CVs from a very different point of view. The CVs were not really all that bad but lacked some skills or the other that the company required at that point of time. There was a mismatch of skill requirements and skills available. She felt that she could do something to bridge that gap. She says, 'After that, I started talking to a few companies and a few clients and eventually, I came across a company from Singapore which was looking for people with certain skills and I could provide the people with those skills.' And that is where it all started.

Rajshri started The Catalyst in 1998, and operated the firm single-handedly from the outhouse of her parents' bungalow. From the very start, she was determined to provide quality service to all her clients and focus only on Information Technology. It was the time of IT boom in Pune which proved to be a boon for her firm. In fact, she said that her firm has worked with almost all the big IT houses that began setting up their development centres in and around Pune at that time. Rajshri adds that recruitment at the entry levels are usually not outsourced, so she decided that her dealings should be mostly in the middle and top levels only. This helped her firm to focus on one domain and function within a defined scope. Over a period of two to three years she had a team of seven people working with her.

When asked whether she faced competition from other similar recruitment firms initially, she said that there were quite a few recruitment firms, but most of them did not understand the IT needs from a recruitment point of view. Also, there were others who used to function only during the heavy recruitment seasons and disappear during the rest of the year. They lacked reliability and focus. This proved to be a big strength for The Catalyst, which stayed with its clients through thick and thin, delivering value whenever required.

So, was this venture all about making the most of positives? She said, 'It is never just an upside curve. There are always ups and downs. I had too many challenges. But those challenges only turned into opportunities. I was on my own. and many times, didn't know what I was doing. It was not like I am raw and new. I knew the companies, I knew whom to approach, what to sell and how to sell. I had the whole background and eventually, it got converted into good things for me. It's not like I had contacts in the IT industry but that industry being a happening one back then helped me.' Then came the crash. 'It is these years which taught us that IT should not be our only focus and we learned to get into other fields.'

The Catalyst now provides recruitment solutions to other sectors too and has expanded into employability enhancement training as well. Rajshri proudly talks about it, 'We identify the need of the Corporates and train job seekers in the required technical and soft skills which make them employable and productive resource from day one. Even after all these years, she still works with a small team of less than twenty who manage clients from different sectors.

Rajshri strongly believes that an entrepreneur is born. 'I can't push my ideas on anybody else. I can't expect anyone else to pursue my idea and make it big,' she adds. She attributes her success to a bit of everything. One needs passion and a stroke of luck as well. One must dream of what one wants to achieve day in and day out. One must open up and explore everything one can be, realize one's complete potential. She believes that a person exists on this planet for 70 or 80 years, and during that time every person should do as much as possible, play as many roles as he or she can and bloom like a flower.

Family or related stress should not be allowed to meddle with your focus. However, she stresses that family is exceptionally important. Whenever she is with the family, she gives them her complete attention and time. In her own words, 'It has to be outer success and inner happiness, both. Being an entrepreneur, I have the flexibility that people swiping their cards in at 9 in the morning don't. And this helps me have a balanced life.'

When asked what her family's stance was towards her venture, Rajshri smiles and says, 'Initially, as it was a new idea, they didn't know much and they didn't bother too. But now, my husband (who is a chartered accountant by profession) has realized that I am doing something worthwhile and he is interested and supportive. I guess this realization happened while I bought my first car within short span of running The Catalyst.'

For those who would like to start something of their own, she has a few words. 'We don't learn much from textbooks. You can't learn how to swim by reading a book on how to swim. Similarly, you have to get into entrepreneurship to learn about it. It's not advisable to start something very late—40 is still fine. Sometimes, the physical running around is just too much.' The idea may have come from one person, but a good team will help in executing that idea and support you through the various phases of growth and decline.

One should be completely prepared and wait for an opportunity to come by, and when it does, not to waste it. When starting something new, never be afraid of failures. Patience and perseverance are the qualities that will see you through.

Usually, people are in love with the whole thought of having something of their own, being their own boss, not having to answer to anyone at all but are not ready for the hard work that one needs to put in. Sometimes, they forget that the most crucial thing for any entrepreneurial venture is the customer. One needs to understand them and to keep them happy. One must accept the fact that the customer is the real boss.

Although many people may be of the opinion that an HR consultancy is just CV passing, once in the business, many realize that it is much more than that. It's knowing what the customer wants and what you can deliver. Her favourite mantra in this regard is 'Always under-promise and over-deliver.'

Rajshri likes to be a part of the solution instead of the problem. She admits that many friends, colleagues, family members come to her for advice often, and she tries to help them out in whatever big or small way possible. Hardly surprising, since here is a lady who knows her job.

SUCCESS MANTRAS

Rajshri runs The Catalyst with a very simple formula which according to her has been instrumental in the success and growth of her firm. She calls them the three Cs: Commitment, Challenge and Change. She believes that one must be committed to one's clients and provide honest and the best possible service consistently. Second, should be open to challenges and curious about the hidden opportunities in problematic situations. Finally, she strongly agrees that change is the only constant in today's world. And only those who can adapt to change at the pace of the change itself, will survive and flourish. Rajshri deals with all her clients honestly and maintains high levels of transparency in her transactions. She believes that one's clients gradually get to know that you are a good businessperson to deal with. One cannot keep the clients in the dark forever. Someday they will find out and that will be the end of it.

SAMEER DESAI
Seagull Advertising

Sameer Desai says that being an entrepreneur need not be as lucrative as working in a corporate job. As the head of a successful advertising and brand consulting company, however, he believes that being on one's own is the best way to be.

∽

FLIGHT OF ENTERPRISE

Vishwesh R., Pranay Gupta and Sampanna Kagalkar

It is said that one learns the most during adversity. Not many would understand this better than Sameer Desai. Starting from scratch with no business background, leaving a prestigious job and choosing an uncharted path fraught with many unknowns, facing detractors and instilling confidence in them by doing good work, and finally, dealing with the mighty blows of recession, this person has been through it all. And needless to say, he has emerged much stronger.

Sameer heads an advertising and brand consulting company called Seagull Advertising. After passing out from SIBM Pune in 1992, he worked in the corporate sector for four years before nurturing Seagull whose Wings-for-Profit (W4P) process enables almost any product or service to connect to a profit opportunity. Reflecting on his past, he recalls, 'Everyone has a "garage story". You look at Narayan Murthy or any other successful person who has made it on his own. While I was in school, I used to bind books for the library in the summer vacations. My dad's garage was my den and earning money this way gave me an adrenaline rush like nothing else did.' Setting up ice-cream stalls during Navratras and doing photography at functions were some other areas where he tested the waters.

After completing his MBA, Sameer joined Tata Press and

enjoyed corporate life for four years. The thought of venturing on his own had been at the back of his mind. But neither did he know the timeframe, nor had he any specific ideas. Perhaps 10 years of working for a corporate was what he expected before he framed his own plan of action, he says. But destiny had something else in store for him.

'The year I joined Tata Press, they launched the Yellow Pages, and I was involved with it. After we completed it, the experience we got in the direct marketing domain helped us launch a Database Services business. As things were going pretty well, I got an offer to join a McCann subsidiary and I was considering that as an option. This was when a friend of mine at Sterling Resorts asked me to help them do face-to-face engagement with the customers. Promotion through consumer activations was what every multinational company was doing in India in 1996–97. The economy had opened its doors to enterprises abroad, and business in India suddenly seemed a lot easier.' This is how Seagull Advertising and Branding Solutions was born.

Sameer Desai maintains that in India, when you decide to start out on your own, your family background can make or break the whole situation. If you are from a family of entrepreneurs or even from a business family, it might not be that difficult for you. But if you are from a service background, you are in for trouble. Fortunately for him, although his dad might not have wholeheartedly embraced Sameer's decision, he did not oppose it either. 'If you want to do it, you do it. Worst case, and you still have a roof over your head,' that is what he told him. Even Sameer weighed the risk from all aspects. 'An opportunity had presented itself to me. I liked it. The work was not very capital-intensive. I had made some savings which could be of use, and I thought that I was young and could always come back to corporate life if things did not work out well. That was it. I did not think of it beyond this and took the plunge.'

'In the eyes of society, even today, a venture of your own pales in front of the heavily paying jobs that are offered on your campuses,' he says. 'You have to expect an explosive reaction from your parents—no less. It's like a flock of seagulls. They will tell you this cannot be done, things are never done this way, it's not in your blood, you cannot do it—all kinds of things to dishearten you. You have to be strong.'

But he says that your family is generally the most difficult to convince, only because they love you more than anyone else. 'Whenever you have two paths, one known and one unknown, anyone who is your well-wisher, and that includes your family, friends and relatives, will tell you to take the known path, and this is only because they love you. They do not want you to take the unknown path only because they want you to be successful. They want you to be safe, they want you to be happy. And they oppose you only because they have not seen success in what you want to do. Had they seen that, they might have done it themselves. So the onus is not on them to support you, but on you to prove to them that the path you have chosen is the right one for you.'

Before 2002, Seagull was mostly about helping clients with consumer activations and promotions. With time, Sameer realized that there is not a particularly thick line between suggesting and planning out promotional activities for a client and creating advertisements on similar lines with similar ideas.

'It was a natural extension. But with time, I further thought that not everyone needs to advertise to become a brand. So that's how I moved towards branding. It was a move towards an integrative approach where we provide across-the-board solutions for a client to build a stronger brand.'

Sameer Desai admitted that with Seagull, he has not yet reached a place where he can think about expanding his business geographically. 'There is still some way to go to start thinking about expanding or venturing into new verticals. The years from 2002 to 2007 were wonderful. There was optimism everywhere, business was plentiful and growth was tremendous. We at Seagull bought the whole office space you see around you. We bought a lot other assets. The banks were willing.' But in 2008, recession hit really hard. That was when matters started to go wrong and agencies found their clients cutting down on their advertising expenses, thus leading to loss of business for Seagull. Banks also cut down their credit limits, which led to a cash crunch.

But there has been positive learning as well. 'We have become much stronger after the recession because we were forced to take a fresh look at our structures and systems.'

Talking about expansion plans, Sameer rebuffs the importance attached to a pan-India geographical presence to be called a national-level ad agency. 'If we can get more clients from different parts of the country, I would see that as an expansion. Today, the internet allows us to be at one place and service our clients who live in far-off places. So I don't know if I want to be physically present at different places, but it would be good to service diverse markets, and these one can find in plenty within India.'

There are different traits of an entrepreneur. 'What worked for me might not work for someone else. There are some people who venture into entrepreneurship only after they have a reputation in their work, their industry. In such a case, it becomes easier as one has all the contacts and a good amount of networking already exists. The skill-set required for such a business is also well-honed.

'But for me, more than anything else, it was perseverance. At times, just being there was all that mattered. Does it mean that I can be dumb and be there? No, it's not possible. Can I just sit there and not work hard? No, that is not possible. Can I be there and not update my skill-sets? No, that is not possible either. So my solution to the problem is just being there. I believe that one day you will get that ball to hit a six. But then you have to be ready to face that ball. You cannot say that when the ball comes, then I will think about it. So you have to work hard, be consistent and wait for that opportunity. It will surely come your way.'

Why do businesses fail? That's a very commonly asked question. 'It's not necessarily because the idea lacks quality, but because the cash flows don't match. If I cannot pay my bills at the end of this month, I will have to shut down. Do clients in India pay bills on time? Never! If a client does not pay you, can you take them to court? You can, but you might get your money after 10 years. So one thing I learnt is to make sure that you clear your bills at the end of each month. Do not chase clients in a terrain where money is dicey,' he reflects. 'For a professional service like ours, the biggest challenge is brand acceptance. Credibility is what sustains a business.'

Isn't maintaining a work–life balance a very difficult task for a first-generation entrepreneur? 'It's a common notion that being an entrepreneur, you won't get time for your family life. I don't think that's true. I see many of my friends in the corporate jobs who travel 15–20 days in a month. It's not all black and white. There are phases. For example, for us, the initial few months were the most trying times. Then, over the years, as the brand gained credibility, it got better. Then recession was another time when everything became difficult. So there are phases, and these phases can be a part of every corporate—there can be releases, downturns or bad patches for the companies during which time they make their employees work very hard. So I think it is the whole sector which has to go through these ups and downs, whether you work for yourself or for someone else.'

But sustaining the entrepreneurial spirit is the most cumbersome of all tasks. 'There are times when you are in the red and at the end of a tiresome day, you ask yourself—what the hell are you doing all this for? At such times, perseverance comes to the rescue. Keeping an eye on the bigger picture is what saves the day.

'Are my friends in corporate jobs doing any better financially? May be they are. Do they not face problems of their own? You bet they do. Do I miss being in their place, having missed out on something? I don't. Maybe I don't know what I am missing. Ignorance is bliss. Do they miss being in my position? Every single day! Most of them would give their left arm to have a well-established business of their own today. But a lot of them can't. I think they lost when they got too used to the good times.'

One of the best things about being an entrepreneur, according to Sameer Desai, is that you are your own boss. No one can shout at you, and ask you not to do things your way. When you have a boss, you have to apply all kinds of diplomatic skills to wade through the murky waters of office politics if you want to be noticed. But here, you can afford to stick to your own ethos, even when it does not go down well with the client. What's the worst that can happen? The client can break all ties with you. But you would still have a roof over your head. And above all, you would have your dignity and self-respect intact.'

For Sameer Desai, entrepreneurship involves a series of events taking place at different points of time, affected by different variables—time, economic, situational and shaped by the human touch. Entrepreneurship is not about a sudden idea that changes everything. 'First, the idea has to connect to something that you really want to do. Second, you have to see if there is an opportunity in the market and if the customer needs to be served. Third, what is the competitive level that you are going to face. If all these three things fit in, you've got your eureka moment.'

In his domain of business, Sameer agrees that every day he sees many of his clients come across their so-called eureka moments. Seagull's Wings-for-Profit is a process which, through special brainstorming and discussion, helps bring out a whole bag of ideas. 'There are many times, at such occasions, when the client asks me why I don't take an equity share in the company, since the idea was suggested by us and wanting to invest in the new company would be but natural. But I do not see Seagull there as yet. There is still some distance to go. Business ideas are very difficult to implement—you need to have the whole nine yards in place. Creative ideas are very different. We work in a creative space and you just need a few resources to execute creative ideas vis-à-vis business ideas.'

'So for an entrepreneur, an idea is not sufficient. You have to structure your way through it. You might get many routes, and you might have to test the routes one by one. But one thing is certain—you have to go ahead by cutting all the ropes of the past. You cannot do it half-heartedly. You have to just go. If you do that, you will succeed.'

Sameer insists that if one is in a privileged position, it is one's duty to support such people who are not. There are no two ways about it. 'An organization like ours does not need to score brownie points with the government as we are not affected by the government. We at Seagull get opportunities wherein we can help organizations with a social objective by putting up a communication channel together which can help them achieve their objective. I don't think there is anything wrong with having a commercial objective if you are socially responsible.'

For instance, Seagull has a client who recycles paper and converts them into notebooks. 'We helped them create this business and also developed for them a programme where 5 per cent of the returns from each notebook go towards the notebooks for lesser privileged children. Today, they are supporting 10,000 children. They take care of the annual requirements of notebooks for these children and we feel proud in having helped them do it. So I would say being socially responsible is no longer a choice. You do it because you live in this world and you want it to be a better place—for me it's as simple as that.'

'In my business, unless I have experience, why should the clients trust me? It's all about trust, and that comes only through experience and not through money. Money is a by-product.'

'In life, you might face choices—maybe a company to work for, a location to work out of, or a product to work towards. If you have to choose something, choose your boss.'

'When you get a job, get a roof over your head as soon as possible. Once that is there, nothing else matters. You won't have to do things you don't want to do. Even if you are losing in business, if every client of yours ditches you, at the end of the day you will still have a roof over your head. I realized the value of this adage during the recession.'

Sameer Desai maintains that MBA is important today when the herd mentality is very visible. Business is a challenging environment. Here, you need someone who has had a variety of exposure and a good overview of the different aspects of a business. 'Even if you are an entrepreneur, does an MBA help? Of course it does. You get to have an understanding of more than just one field. For example, an engineer may not have the perspective of how the supply chain, production, operations and marketing and sales are interlinked. This is what an MBA gives to you—an all-round business perspective.'

But he insists that it is important that an MBA education is imbibed in a proper fashion. If it's just about getting a degree and getting a well-paying job, it's useless. You don't need education to be successful. You need skills.' According to Sameer Desai, therefore, an MBA is not a prerequisite for being successful in a corporate life or even as an entrepreneur. But it helps for sure.

SUCCESS MANTRAS

'When the going is good, it is easy to believe that one can never fail, and that business will always be there. Develop new products and services that can add value to your offerings. Train yourself to spot opportunities. An organization has to learn to live within its means. Savings are as crucial as cash flows.'

www.ingramcontent.com/pod-product-compliance
Lightning Source LLC
Chambersburg PA
CBHW020639220526
45464CB00001B/212